Bending Water

Valuing a child's point of view

Suzanne Geier & Wendy Potter

ISBN 979-8-9999020-0-9

Independently published

Geier & Potter
Melbourne FL

Interior and Cover design by LifeArtStuff Creative Studio

First edition, September 2025

Printed in the United States of America

10 9 8 7 6 5 4 3 2 1

"**Bending Water is a history of the Brevard Community College Lab School. But it is much more than that.** Using lessons learned at the Lab School, authors Suzanne Geier and Wendy Potter emphasize how important parent-child bonding is to a child's development and how that development is enhanced by understanding, nurturing, and engagement. Those same lessons greatly enrich the parenting experience."

John Antoon II, United States District Judge, Middle District of Florida

"**Once upon a time, I lived a concept that made my life an interesting and long-term learning experience. It was called Lab School.** It was a place for parents and children to learn to think, act, and talk, so we all grew. This beautiful book, so well organized, could be a blueprint for recreating this wonderful program."

Betsy Baughan, M.A. LMHC

"**Great memories! Well-organized presentation...informative** to the reader. Particularly found info on social/emotional development helpful."

Pete Riebsame, PhD, ABPP

This book is dedicated to the many children and their parents, whom we had the good fortune of watching and supporting as they explored the vast opportunities in life.

We treasure the memories and experience.

Table of Contents

The goal of education is not to increase the amount of knowledge but to create the possibilities for a child to invent and discover..."

Jean Piaget

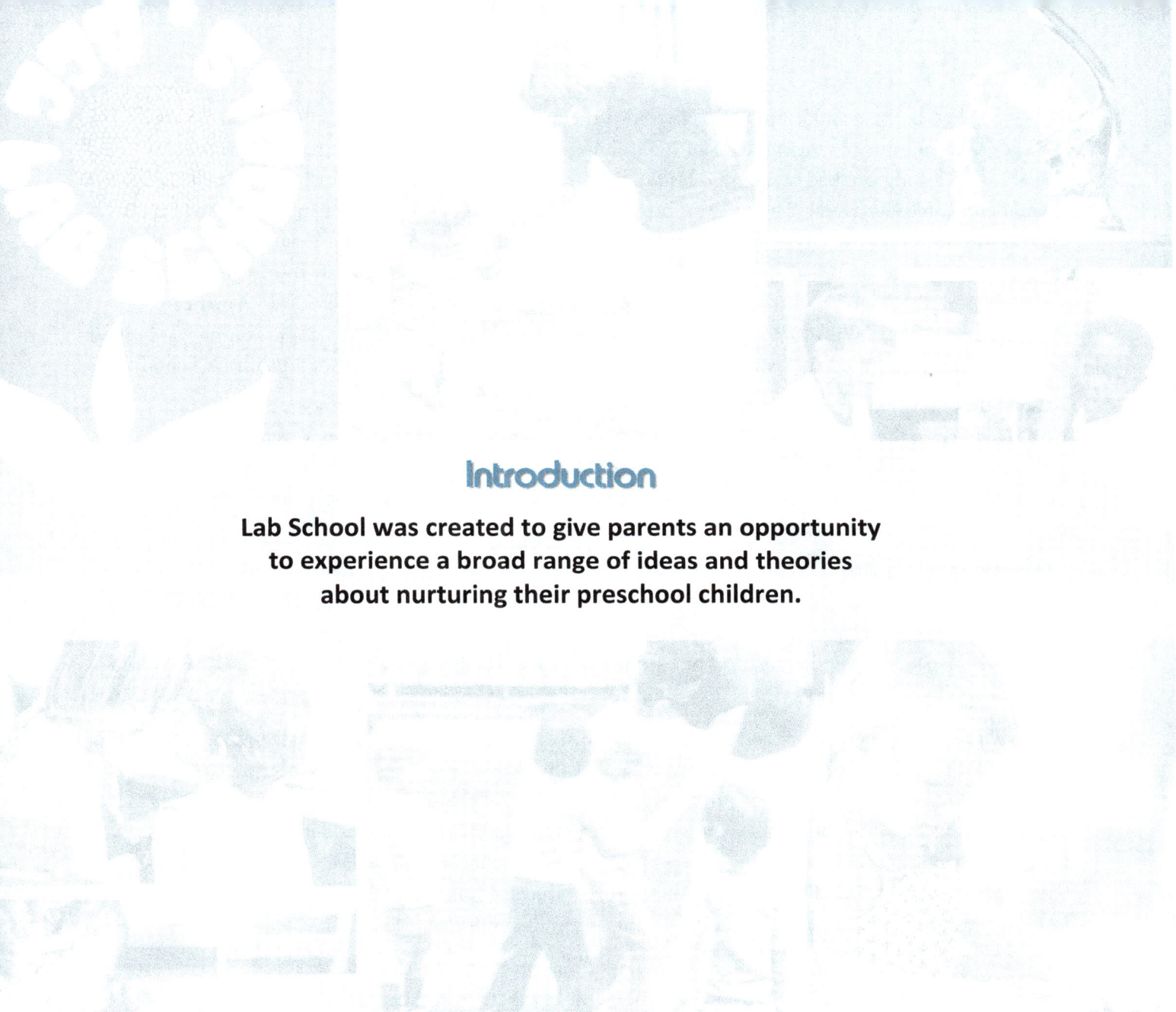

Introduction

Lab School was created to give parents an opportunity to experience a broad range of ideas and theories about nurturing their preschool children.

When Barbara and John Young arrived at their new home in Cocoa Beach, Florida, they found a community changing. It was 1966. John's job with the Boeing Corporation in Seattle, Washington, had transferred him to Brevard County in Florida to work at the Kennedy Space Center and Cape Canaveral. The area was buzzing with the excitement of rocket launches into space, the moon, and beyond. With a booming population coming from many states and foreign countries, Brevard County was changing from an economy based on citrus, cattle farming, and a few tourists to a technological hub of companies like Boeing, McDonald Douglas, Martin-Marietta, Pan American, Aerodyne, and Pratt-Whitney, and a local engineering firm called Radiation. Air conditioning was limited. Some corporations added an "extra-hardship" stipend for employees living in these "primitive" conditions.

New houses, shopping centers, roads, and bridges were to be built to replace wooden bridges and causeways across the Indian River Lagoon, the Banana River, and Sebastian Inlet. Over time, the new public schools were named Satellite and Astronaut High Schools and Gemini and Freedom Elementary Schools. New residents staffed new hospitals and businesses, attracted by the space center and the community's new business and job opportunities.

Brevard County's uncrowded rivers and Atlantic beaches attracted surfers, fishermen, sailors, and space center workers. In 1966, three weekly local county newspapers were consolidated to create a daily newspaper, *Brevard Today*. Al Neuharth had arrived as the new head of Gannett Florida and had created this new newspaper. Several years later, he used the format of the Brevard County newspaper to develop *USA Today*.

Along with the new elementary and secondary schools, educational opportunities in Brevard were growing. Continuing education for space workers became available at Brevard Engineering College, which, in 1966, was renamed Florida Institute of Technology, a research university that granted advanced degrees. Brevard Community College, a two-year junior college, had a new president in 1968, Dr. Maxwell King, who supported Barbara Young's ideas for the Lab School. The college received support from the federal government to enrich community support for education and mental health, and the Florida legislature authorized what became "adult education" in the junior colleges.

The "can-do spirit" of the space explorers and Barbara's experience as a clinical psychiatric social worker inspired her creation of the Lab School, an opportunity for parents to experience a broad range of ideas and theories for nurturing their preschool children. Barbara Young sought a preschool for their youngest son but did not find any like the one she had known in Seattle, which focused on children's play as the desired vehicle for early learning. She envisioned a comprehensive parent-child program structured as an adult educational program for new parents, with a morning preschool for parents and children, and an evening class for parents. She convinced the new president to include this adult education program in the college curriculum.

The concept of school rooms as laboratories for prospective teachers was not new. Colleges and Universities traditionally created laboratory schools using "best practices" in teaching. Experienced instructors were models for college students training to be K-12 educators. Similarly, BCC Lab School trained parents, their children's first and most important teachers, guided by Parent Educators and Early Childhood Teachers during evening and daytime classes. Barbara considered parents to be the children's most important teachers and required that they attend the lab school parent classes and the children's daytime classes. The program attracted many new Brevard residents who were largely isolated from the traditional support of friends and extended family as they raised their young children. Parents paid a modest tuition for the non-credit classes that trained them to assist in classes attended by their preschool children. BCC Lab School was born. Churches in the community rented their Sunday School classrooms for the morning preschool.

In the following chapters, we describe everyday life in Lab School classes. The Lab School story includes many moments when children and adults recognized developmental processes and included children in resolving problems presented in the children's growing physical, emotional, social, and cognitive skills and needs.

Here is one of those moments when an older toddler (almost three years old) taught us about his physical efforts, emotional needs, problem-solving, and thinking while working at "*bending water.*"

Drinking fountains were often found in or near the Sunday school classrooms. A step stool enabled the children to get drinks of water independently.

Three-year-old Robbie stood on the top step, pushed the lever, and watched the stream of water rising from the faucet. He looked and looked. He could see the water was too far away to reach with his mouth; he was not tall enough.

A Parent Educator noticed Robbie's efforts to get a drink. He had moved his left hand behind the water streaming and rising from the spigot, attempting to move the stream toward his mouth. On observing Robbie and curious about his efforts, the Parent Educator asked, "What are you doing?" He replied, "I'm bending the water so I can get a drink." The adult asked, "Is it working?" "Not yet," was his answer. "Well, if you would like, we can get a cup and you can fill that up."

Any moment in a child's day brings opportunities for solving problems. This optimistic youngster had an observant and nurturing adult who offered him a choice as he recognized the problem of water that didn't "bend" so that he could get a drink.

- She protected his growing sense of power by knowing that he could choose to get a drink of water all by himself and that he was aware of how a drinking fountain works.
- She permitted him to evaluate how it worked without diminishing his effort.
- Then she offered him an alternative, the power to choose another way to satisfy his thirst: solve a problem.

When adults in a preschool child's life nurture a child's growing body and mind with empathy and information appropriate for the child's developing body and mind, children begin to know their individuality in the larger world beyond their family and to trust the guidance of adults to get their needs met. Parents and extended family members, babysitters, teachers, daycare providers, and other adults who provide childcare for their employees' children may find helpful information in the following chapters about new ways to nurture and enhance the development of society's youngest generation.

Barbara Young's focus on children and parents growing together included exploration of the expanding research in human development and traditional theories in the neurosciences, psychology, medicine, sociology, and education. As Parent Educators, what we learned from our experience in Lab school, along with the children and parents, has proven timeless. We tell the story of Lab School in response to those parents in the program during the late 1960s and beyond who are now grandparents. These grandparents wonder where their children, now parents themselves, might find the type of support for their parenting during the preschool years they knew in the Lab School program, which no longer exists. The college's support for the program seemed to wane as the college grew and ultimately became a four-year institution.

Cultural changes in mass communication, new occupational choices, and the COVID pandemic have led us to record our memories of the challenge Barbara Young presented in our role as Parent Educators. We are writing this book for anyone who loves and respects children and their parents and seeks to help children learn as valued participants in problem-solving. In the following chapters, we describe everyday life in Lab School classes. The Lab School story includes many moments when children and adults recognized developmental processes and included children in resolving problems presented in the children's growing physical, emotional, social, and cognitive skills and needs.

An effective early childhood program enhances the brain's ability to perceive, remember, and motor plan."

Barbara Young

Chapter 1 | Daily Life in Lab School

*"A parent is the child's first and best teacher.
Don't miss some of life's sweetest pleasures or crucial moments,
as the baby grows from infant to child."*

Burton White, Ph.D., *The First Three Years*, 1976

What to Expect on a Visit to Lab School
A Look at the Environment Shaping Children's Growth and Development

The first Lab School opened in 1969 in Cocoa Beach at the Riverside Presbyterian Church, where the Sunday School classrooms became the home of the morning preschool. Each Lab School that opened in the coming years was located in churches in different communities along what became known as the Space Coast. Lab School grew to encompass eight additional locations: Titusville, Cocoa, Rockledge, Merritt Island, Satellite Beach, Melbourne, Palm Bay-East, and Palm Bay-West.

Parents became avid recruiters as they came to value their own experience and as other churches recognized the value of educating parents. The program initially enrolled parents and their preschool children ages three to five; infant and toddler classes were added later.

The first step in organizing the school was to create spaces for diverse types of play with toys and equipment typical of pre-school settings. These "centers" focused on physical movements, emotional and social experiences, and learning to think and create. Creative and typical use of the toys and media occurred in perceptual activities, memory building, and pretend play.

Each church provided several Sunday school rooms. The furniture in the rooms often included child-sized tables and chairs and perhaps some bookshelves. The school could use the church furniture to create the "Centers" of activity. Every Lab School had the same centers with similar equipment. The Boeing Corporation provided seed money for some of the equipment.

Adults and children left all equipment and materials used during the school day well-organized in the centers at the end of the day. If the churches requested, the school equipment might be covered for the weekend; the Sunday school teachers were welcome to use the school equipment. Furniture would be arranged as the church requested. The parents cleaned the school every Friday.

Block Center

Shelves that stored "kindergarten" wooden blocks of many sizes, other blocks of wood or heavy cardboard, toy cars, trucks, animals, and people. Play was typically on the floor, with a large area spread out for play while building with the blocks. Creative and pretend block-building efforts were often accompanied by play.

Perception Center

A table generally contained shelves filled with books, puzzles, games, and sometimes musical instruments with color-coded instruction cards. Visual, auditory, and tactile sensory activities, planning, and memory were some of the developmental processes accompanying perceptual activities.

Housekeeping

A child-sized kitchen with pans, dishes, utensils, stove, shelves, and a table with chairs; dolls and stuffed animals; and dress-up clothes for pretend and dramatic play. Parents often added items reflecting their child's interests in pretend play.

Art Center

There was a large table with child-sized chairs and shelves containing various media, including crayons, markers, paints, playdough, easels, and large and small brushes. Creative use of the materials was encouraged.

Outdoor Playground

The playground featured swings, a slide, a jungle gym, a sandbox, climbing equipment, a water table, and riding toys. This environment supported both fine and gross motor skills development, promoting efficient physical movement while laying a sensory and cognitive foundation essential for overall development.

Obstacle Course

Set up in a hallway or on the playground with a variety of opportunities to crawl, jump, hop, walk a balance beam, ladders, cardboard boxes for crawling in different ways, all providing the planning and sequences of physical behaviors.

Collaborative Roles in the School Community
How Educators, Parents, and Children Shaped the Learning Environment

The children and adults, both educators and parents, had well-defined roles in Lab School. Parent training for their roles began during the first parent class of the school year. Each staff member explained their Lab School responsibilities. New parents were both apprehensive and curious about the expectations of their role in the school.

The Early Childhood Teacher's role in Lab School differed somewhat from her earlier experience as a teacher in kindergarten or preschool classes. Rather than directing the children's activities, she joined the children in their choice of play, modeling a supportive relationship with the children. Some parents grew into the teacher role after their own Lab School children went to kindergarten. The children recognized the teacher's special role as the adult present every school day. She also organized equipment and made monthly calendars and lesson plans with the center assignments for parents on their workday. She organized field trips and "Working Parent or Fathers' Days," usually on a Saturday, when each child came with the parent who could not have a regular workday during the week.

Parent Educators were master's degree-level professional social workers, psychologists, mental health and guidance counselors, and nurses. Their role in Lab School's daytime children's classes was to collaborate closely with Early Childhood Teachers in training the parents on the many ways to support the children's play.

Parent evening classes led by Parent Educators included information from noted authorities on child and human development, whose theories and practices were useful as parents began to understand the adult role in the school and as parents. They taught and modeled a problem-solving approach during all morning and evening class times. In every parent class, questions arose that recognized the rules and relationships related to problems among and between children and adults. Adults made observations of the children's play activities. The observations provided a snapshot of a child's behavior during play and interactions with other children. Parent Educators, Early Childhood Teachers, and parents all observed the unique developmental levels of each of the 3–5-year-old children, guided and recorded on the Developmental Task Inventory (DTI) created by Barbara Young (*see Appendix*)

Parent Educators also led evening parent classes for Infant and Toddler Class parents and their Lab School morning class, where parents discussed individual questions about their child's and family's developmental needs. The Parent Educators organized the morning classes for the Toddler and Infant classes similarly to the role of the Teacher for the 3–to 5-year-old children.

Barbara Young valued the training of all adults who were a part of Lab School. She required all Parent Educators to have proper educational backgrounds, master's level psychology, social work or counseling degrees. Of more importance were personal characteristics and personality traits. She often expressed the view that you could always add training; it is not easy to add personality traits. Warmth, intelligence, curiosity, adaptability, dependability, organizational skills, compassion, and firmness were all necessary, Barbara believed, as one interacts with young children. Parents also responded to those traits and learned to demonstrate them in their work with all the children, not just their own.

Lab School teachers often had college training as early childhood teachers but also came from the ranks of experienced Lab School's parents whose children had moved into elementary school. Teachers organized the centers for play during the school day as well as to support the choices available to meet the children's needs, including field trips and special occasions. "Backwards Day" on April 1 was one special occasion when creative thinking included clothes turned inside out, snack to begin the day, opposites, whatever the parents and children might invent that was safe different.

The role of the parents was new for both the educators and parents; on visiting a school, one might not recognize what role any adult was fulfilling, educator or parent! All adults respected the children's choices, supported their play and helped them solve problems. Parents were relieved to serve in this supportive role rather than having a disciplinary role. Their experience with their parent role was in the beginning stages.

Both mothers and fathers were registered by the college in the BCC Lab School Parent Education class and paid tuition as students in the non-credit adult education class. They also were billed a modest fee by the college for the children who were enrolled in the morning preschool classes. Handbooks for parents were developed that outlined specific requirements for parents participating in the program. (See Appendix for *Lab School Guidebook for Parents*).

The families came from a broad cross-section of our community, people with and without college degrees, in professions, businesses, education, and the trades. They came from many of our United States, Jamaica, India, Great Britain, Thailand, Ireland, Scotland, France, Germany, Latvia, Puerto Rico, Haiti, the

Bahamas, and the Solomon Islands. Brevard County and the space center had developed quite a diverse population!

One parent from every family was required to attend all evening classes and one weekly daytime class; often, both parents attended the evening class together. Typically, the mother was the parent who attended the morning class to assist the Early Childhood Teacher. The children attended their class every day it was in session. Some mothers had full-time careers before becoming parents, some managed both full and part time work after their children were born and still found a way to be a part of a Lab School morning workday. Occasionally a child's babysitter or nanny or even a grandparent became part of the morning sessions. Several times a year a weekend morning class enabled attendance by parents who could not attend during the day, typically fathers. Each father, regardless of his occupation, managed his schedule to learn for the benefit of himself and his family. They included retail clerks, secretaries, attorneys, physicians, pharmacists, teachers, business owners, tradesmen, accountants, engineers, fisherman, artists, writers, nurses, a broad spectrum of occupations and education and nationalities!

Parents often created and volunteered extra time in the school on a Saturday when they painted classrooms, built or refurbished new playground equipment, and repaired or added to the fencing around playgrounds. The group planned and enjoyed this experience, bonding and enjoying one another's company, ending with a joint sense of pride and accomplishment. The host churches also appreciated these contributions to their facility and often provided indoor space beyond their initial agreement. There were many ways the parents recognized how the school was working for their whole family. They valued their role in the school.

Lab School's parents of the 3- to 5-year-old children recognized that what they were learning about the development of both children and parents would have been especially valuable during their child's earlier years. They lobbied for the college to expand the ages for Lab School to include Infant and Toddler classes for children from birth to age three. Another addition was a five-day option for four-year-old children which began several years after the first school was opened. The host churches also recognized the value of the new programs and offered an additional room for the infant class.

A maximum of twenty preschoolers were enrolled in the morning 3–5-year-old preschool class; ten or twelve children in each infant and toddler class, which met one day each week. The children would arrive with their parent and spend 2 ½ to 3 hours at school. In the 3–5-year-old class, four to six parents would stay one day each week, what we called their "workday" on Monday, Wednesday or Friday. When a five day program was created for the older 4- and 5-year-old children on Tuesday and Thursday, parents of the older children would spend an additional day to assist the teacher.

Every day the children of all ages in the Lab School made choices about their play during their school day. The playground was often the first area available for the older children's play, but as soon as all the adults working that day arrived, several other centers of play would be open and available to the children. The 3-5-year-old children engaged in a wide choice of play opportunities with support from adults, typically one adult in each "center." A time for mid-morning snacks was the only activity when the whole group was together.

Play is the work of the child. Choices of play available to the children motivated independence and learning at each child's level of development and interests. The essence of a play-based preschool experience lies in the child's power to make and manage their choices and bodies, to have the power of self-control. For example, the ability to pump a swing is a skill many 3-5-year-old children seek to learn. They might choose to swing some time every day to gain confidence in their physical movements. Adults might suggest and demonstrate different ways to use their legs in the pumping motion. Communication among children and adults about taking turns on the swing added language to the activity.

All adults observed and supervised the children's choices, respecting and guiding a child's emerging physical development, awareness of others, emotional expressions, language development, communication, motivation, interests, and temperament. These subjects of parent education will be explored more fully in subsequent chapters related to children's physical, emotional/social, and cognitive development.

Barbara Young's background as a psychiatric social worker led her to appreciate the value of theoretical knowledge as a pathway to understanding human behavior and personality. She was an avid reader, open to new learning, and kept abreast of new insights. She reviewed theorists and introduced to parents the ideas of Piaget, Erikson, Maslow, Thomas, Chess, Ayres, Braselton, Fraiberg, Galinsky, Greenspan, and Turecki. In later chapters, you will learn more about these theorists who added valuable information to parents' understanding of the opportunities and techniques Lab School modeled as they worked and played during school time with the children. Faculty were also learning about current research and theories.

A parent class preceded the first day of school for the children. The parents had many questions about fulfilling their role in the classrooms. The parents were encouraged to talk to their child about what would happen when they went to Lab School. On the first day of school, each mother or father stayed with their child to experience the whole day together. Some recommendations:

1. *Dress for playing; closed shoes are best. Bring a change of clothes in a backpack, which will be available in cubby holes or a hook for hanging the backpack.*
2. *Lab School can be described to the children as a place with other children, parents, and teachers. Children can play with many interesting and different toys and equipment in the classrooms and on the playground. Snacks will be available every day.*
3. *Explain to your child that you will be at school one day every week, and their teacher (say her name) and other parents will be there every day.*
4. *Lab School children can make choices at school about where to play, and they learn how to use the toys and equipment safely.*

The hands-on experiences in the daytime school provided moments for parents to explore ideas about working together and to enhance their understanding of the children's and parents' developmental stages. Adults and children alike were invited to learn from the same premise: we have varying histories, talents, and interests. Our histories and differences may describe how we act; new experiences enable us to learn if our actions work for us, or suggest what we might need, wish to learn, or change.

In the first parent class, Parent Educators discussed that there would be conflicts among the children and adults. Recognizing problems related to any new experience does not make them disappear; humans need to find common ground for meeting any problem or challenge. Safety was a priority. Barbara believed that continual awareness of one's own personality and behavior was a key to facilitating one's interactions with other adults and children and as well as within their families.

Barbara recognized that parents and educators needed a working plan and methods for interacting with each other and the children as they assisted the teachers. All parents were experiencing the world of early childhood, mostly for the first time. Evening parent classes were essential if the school provided consistent methods for solving problems and attending to children's needs during the school day. The educators and parents learned and practiced this important role in helping children learn how to solve problems related to their physical, emotional/social, and cognitive experiences.

Problem-solving moments sought to expand the choices available to parents and children. The goal of the parent education program was to respect a family's history and each child's unique talents within some simple boundaries for safety and exploration. A child's choices during the school day provided opportunities for all to learn about each child's needs and potential as they worked together in the school environment.

1. During the school day, children could choose their activities. Snack time was the only whole-group activity, although a child could choose not to eat the snack.
2. Children could play wherever an adult was available for supervision. Typically, one parent would be stationed in each "center."
3. Hurting others was not allowed; name-calling was discouraged.
4. Problem-solving focused on conflicts and difficulties as they arose, ensuring the physical and emotional safety of all, permitting the children to choose where and how to play, protecting the child's growing powers to solve problems, and meeting any challenge as it arose.

The child's role in Lab School was to make choices about play activities. If the child repeatedly chose any particular area or center for play, that choice still offered new challenges and new skills for their developing body. While the Lab School rules may seem oversimplified and the problem-solving moments took brief periods of time away from the children's play, they both prompted communication and thinking rather than simple consequences or punishment for "breaking" or "testing" a rule, a skill for a lifetime. Children learned to negotiate the use of a toy or equipment. Emotional and physical reactions and discussion regarding the use of school equipment, as well as expressions of disappointment, sadness, or outrage, were acceptable subjects for discussion and problem solving; emotions were named and nurtured. Children and adults became accustomed to talking with each other about important feelings and behaviors, and they discovered the value of addressing problems as they arose.

As we describe the Lab School program, we include observations of children and adults during school days. Our memories of the families growing together are vivid; we observed healthy family and group development as adults experienced the Lab School environment. Many years later, their questions today, seeking the same experience for their adult children and grandchildren, bring new relevance to our efforts to tell the Lab School story. The needs of adults and children may have changed somewhat as our world has changed, but the potential and need for healthy growth within families and associates remains challenging.

Problem-Solving in Playtime
Approaches to Resolving Challenges During Children's Play Activities

Guiding the families through a problem-solving process was important for all the adults during the school day and in the parent classes. The simple process we used involved several steps and is useful in many settings:

1. Identify the problem: Each child or adult involved, or even just observing the problem, offers their awareness.

2. The adult listens and restates or describes what he/she has observed. Others agree there is a problem or need.

3. All participants or observers of the problem may offer ideas. Several solutions may be considered; the choice of a solution is agreed upon.

4. The solution is then implemented and assessed; changes are considered if the first effort or solution doesn't seem to work.

The following chapters describe many moments when this problem-solving practice was used. Every day presented problems, conflicts, and emotions when children's behavior might need some adult guidance. Children became engaged in this process through language that their immature social and cognitive development could understand.

Conflict and Decision-Making Guidance
Parents Gained Confidence and Skills to Navigate Challenging Situations

Often, a child's cry or tears would alert an adult to ask, "What happened?" Moving toward the child, bending down, or sitting on the floor to meet the child's eye level was always the first step when asking, "Are you hurt?"

Comfort and first aid would be provided if needed. The idea that nobody liked getting hurt was expressed. Any child involved or observing was asked to tell what happened and the problem. Children and adults were asked to provide details. The problem solver adult does not offer any opinion except to note there was some conflict or distress and define the problem, repeating the children's words, "He took my car," or "She hit me," or "Help me, I can't get down!"

The next question from the adult: "How do you feel about that?" prompting language with simple words for feelings like "scared, mad, or sad," with the adult expressing feelings as well, especially that nobody likes to get hurt, and getting hurt is no fun for anybody.

Seeing the moment, all children were encouraged to express opinions, emotions, and feelings without any judgment from the adults about whether the feelings were acceptable.

"What can we do about this problem/conflict/pain?"

The adult would ask any child involved or witnessing what happened. It was especially important for any child's point of view to be expressed; any adult might also give more suggestions.

"What can we do the next time this happens?" Again, the adult seeks the children's ideas, recalling school rules about hurting and how they apply to this situation.

"Sharing" is a complex cognitive process that was encouraged, but was a choice a child could make; use of school toys reflected "ownership," unlike the child's own toys at home. Waiting for a turn might be hard; figuring out how two children could play together is also hard. Brainstorming with three-year-old children and a little help from adults was surprisingly productive. Cooperative play begins when an awareness of self-control and power sharing begins.

As they used this problem-solving technique, parents learned to recognize the concepts of protection, permission, and power in their parenting roles.

Their children also began to understand that Lab School's parents and teachers safeguarded each child's safety and learning needs throughout the school day. Following their interests and needs came next. They experienced the power to make choices, communicate with others, have friends, and adapt to change.

Adults, too, became accustomed to communicating with children about problems and safety.

And parents recognized that punishment was not the best solution. The developmental needs of parents and children are a factor in resolving most disagreements. Adults need to forgive children for not knowing how to cooperate, share, not hurt others, and stay safe. Parent's expectations were sometimes altered by other parents whose experiences were different. Children were able to learn those ideals through solving problems that value those attributes from their parents, the most important people in their lives.

Parents came to value their relationships with other parents and educators.

They began to trust different ways to solve problems and to trust that their child's safety and any challenges at school would be nurtured by adults who respected their child's emotions, abilities, and needs. Parents also came to value the opportunity to gain new experiences as they fulfilled their obligations of time and tuition.

Picture right: a parent talking about safety with a child. He pedaled as fast as he could, but he seemed unaware of the others around him.

Supporting Parents Through Education
Parent Classes Tackled Day-to-Day Challenges in the School Environment

Before children came to school, the first parent class introduced parents to their role alongside the other adults. They learned that questions were welcome! Adults wanted to know how to react when aware of a problem. They asked...

What do I do? How do I do it? How do we know it is working? There are many other good questions and problems to solve....

The Parent Educator suggested that parents first become observers of their child to ensure the children's safety and further nurture a child's physical opportunities and challenges, emotional states, social experiences, and thinking skills. Observe the child's choices and how the child seems to be thinking and doing; become aware of and observe your own choices, thoughts, and reactions! Problems could be resolved with respect for the developmental needs of both adults and children. The key was to follow a child's lead. Use language to expand the child's awareness of safety, physical opportunities, social relationships, and simply, to build self-control as the child at play is experiencing and expressing a sense of control. Mental flexibility, social skills and self-discipline are all a part of self-control and crucial for success in academic achievement and everyday life. Responding to a child who asks for help with school equipment, expanding the child's idea of choice, offering alternatives to help solve difficulties with a toy, playground equipment, or another person, the role of all adults was to be present and responsible, and to communicate with others. Solve problems!

Self-awareness activities were offered in the parent classes as an opportunity for parents to become aware of their own response style when problems arise. In one class experience, parents learned different ideas about surprises. They were invited to be aware of their own opinions and reactions at an unexpected moment.

Parent classes were often held in the homes of the Lab School families. To one parent meeting, the Parent Educator brought a laundry basket, well covered by a beach towel, placing it in the center of the parents seated in the living room of the host family. "We'll see...," was her answer to the parent questions about

---

the basket's contents. She knew her family's pet guinea pig in the basket seldom moved around much but hoped that it would move at an unplanned moment.

Indeed, it did! The group was discussing some current school issue, and the mysterious basket had been ignored. Finally, the guinea pig moved, staying within the confines of the basket but with its movement detected as the towel cover moved a bit. Many startled reactions came from the parents: "EEK, WHAT IS THAT!" Some picked their feet off the ground, some exclaimed their original question, with more vigor, some laughed. The Parent Educator then removed the towel to reveal the guinea pig. It had settled into another position. Guinea pigs do not move around much, unlike other small mammals that become pets.

As the parents were invited to examine and explain their startled responses, they gained an awareness of how they deal with the unexpected and surprises. Some were uneasy, some were amused, some fearful, some curious, some angry. Many spoke of an awareness of past experiences with surprises, pets, and sensory issues. Ghosts in the Nursery?!? More about that subject later. Every response was validated.

The group left the meeting amused by the whole series of events! How different we are! The goal of the Parent Educator led to a discussion of empathy for themselves, one another, and their children when confronted by something new, unexpected, or scary. Of course, the guinea pig was unfazed by it all, true to its typical and unflappable guinea pig behaviors and temperament!

Problems associated with daily routines often arose in discussions related to parent duties.

In one school, cleaning tools used by the church custodian were available for use by the parents who mopped the floors on Friday. A string mop was the only type of mop provided by the church at one school, and it prompted a discussion during a night class of the virtues of string mops vs. sponge mops, with ardent proponents of each. The sanitary value, personal preferences, ease of use, relative efficiency--all thoughts and feelings were heard. The issue arose at several meetings. While this seems a trivial issue, it didn't seem trivial to the moms doing the mopping! The Parent Educator and Teacher did not express opinions; this was seen as a problem parents could solve. One mom, somewhat exasperated by the time spent on the discussion, suggested that if anyone needed to bring their own sponge mop to use at school, perhaps the discussion could end. Other issues seemed more important for their time together. The problem never arose again, and the floors were always mopped! Disagreeing was accepted!

Recognizing Stages of Development
A valuable tool for planning activities for young children

Barbara resisted "recipe books" and lesson plans that prescribe how to parent or how to teach parents. She designed a program that nurtured each child and parent's physical, emotional, social, and cognitive skills. She appreciated an individual's unique combination of adult skills and family histories. She drew on her experience and a variety of traditional and contemporary experts whose discoveries about human development became the source of current information for the parents and educators in their Lab School roles. Problem-solving appropriate for a child's level of development or adult's perceptions of needs, rather than any single authority, became the keystone of the Lab School curriculum and the environment offered to families.

This foundation for many Lab School practices was derived from experts whose insights into human growth and development supply some broad descriptions applicable to the development of both parents and children.[1,2] Growth rates, which can vary among individuals, over time, and even within individuals themselves, included the following guidelines:

1. Maturity is reached at different times by different individuals.

2. Different types of growth are interrelated.

3. Each person behaves as though they can achieve their maximum potential, seeking alternatives when primary sources of nurture are unavailable.

4. Specific behaviors arise from more global or general behaviors and become a part of the larger and more complex system from which new specific behaviors develop.

5. Sequences of motor development follow certain directions (head to toe, middle of the body outward, front before back).

6. Orderly sequences of maturation occur naturally for certain behaviors.

---

[1] Papalia, D. E., & Olds, S. W. (1979). *A Child's World: Infancy Through Adolescence*. New York: McGraw-Hill Book Co.
[2] Smart, M., & Smart, R. (1972). *Children: Development and Relationships*. New York: Macmillan.

7. The foundation of growth and development is in the interaction of the child in its environment as the child transforms itself into its mature potential.

8. There are critical times for the development of specific behaviors.

Other sources of educational and psychological theory over the human lifetime were familiar to staff and some parents who had learned about the theories in psychology, education, and business classes. Humanist psychologist Abraham Maslow, PhD, named a series of needs that motivate human behavior. As needs at one level are met, a person is prepared to strive to meet the needs of succeeding levels until the higher order of needs is reached. The ideal, the "self-actualized" person, displays high levels of perception of reality, acceptance of self and others and the natural world, spontaneity, problem-solving ability, self-direction, emotional reaction, frequency of peak experiences, identification with other human beings, satisfying and changing relationships with other people, a democratic character structure, creativity, and a sense of values.

Maslow theorized the following human needs: [3,4]

1. Physiological: for air, food, drink, and rest to achieve balance within the body.

2. Safety: for security, stability, and freedom from fear, anxiety, and chaos, achieved with the help of a structure made up of laws and limits.

3. Belongingness and love or affection and intimacy to be provided by family, friends, and loved ones.

4. Esteem: for self-respect and the respect of others.

5. Self-actualization: a sense that one is doing what one is individually suited for and capable of, to be "true to one's nature."

Expanding Maslow's theory, Psychologist Erik Erikson, PhD, described developmental stages over the lifetime as a series of struggles. Aspects of the struggle, including trial-and-error efforts, lead to perceptions and behaviors for interacting with the world. [5,6]

[3] Maslow, A. H. (1943). *A Theory of Human Motivation*. Originally published in *Psychological Review*, 50, 370-396.
[4] Maslow, A. H. (1954). *Motivation and Personality*. New York: Harper & Brothers.
[5] Erikson, E. H. (1950). *Childhood and Society*. New York: Norton.
[6] Erikson, E. H. (1982). *The Life Cycle Completed*. New York: Norton.

1. Trust vs. Mistrust: Infants and toddlers begin to gain a sense that needs are recognized and met, outweighing the dangers of an unpredictable world. Hope for the future can develop in the child.

2. Autonomy vs. Doubt: Two and three-year-old children gain a sense of autonomy through engaging physical skills with the environment and achieving a goal that enables the child to develop a sense of self-control and willpower.

3. Initiative vs. Guilt: Four- and five-year-old children explore both safely and purposefully as they try out new skills; they gain a new understanding of the problems they encounter as they do so in a safe environment.

4. Industry vs. Inferiority leads to methods and competencies gained during elementary school without a sense of inferiority or guilt.

5. Identity and Role confusion of the adolescent years that lead to a sense of Devotion and Fidelity.

6. Intimacy and Isolation of the young adult years, which can find some resolution through Affiliation and Love, typically found with marriage and parenthood, the stage most Lab School's parents were experiencing.

These broad outlines of human needs and stages of development were presented while orienting parents to the Lab School program and during many parent classes. While parents may have had an awareness of theories about human growth and development, Maslow's and Erikson's theories helped parents recognize that a child's development may not yet have progressed to include the behaviors some parents expected of their child. Parents also learned that their parent/adult role was a new stage for themselves, and other stages were to come.

A significant topic in every parent class brought to the forefront an awareness and understanding of the bond and relationship between each parent and child. The individuality of each parent's bond within their family of origin becomes interwoven with other bonds their new family is developing. A family aware of the value of family relationships can create strong bonds that support belonging, confidence, and optimism at all stages of development.

Not surprisingly, the bond among all the parents in the group became a significant factor in their Lab School experience. A sense of satisfaction and optimism also grew among Lab School's parents and faculty.

Parents came to appreciate how valuable it was for their child to have a variety of trusted adults as a resource for solving problems, major and minor.

Parents were gaining new perspectives and new behaviors to implement in their parenting role. The following conversation among parents depicts what might seem a minor issue. The "put together" parent had solved her own problem that enabled her to arrive at school in an optimistic frame of mind.

"How do you do it?" one mom asked another as they arrived at school one morning. "You are always so 'put together' and on time!" The second mom responded, "Do you see what my children are wearing? (Cotton knit shorts and shirts) They slept in these clothes last night!" "Why didn't I think of that?" said the first mom.

One might think this is a simple problem unless one has had two young children and a schedule a mom seeks to meet. By limiting choices in this instance, she freed herself to meet other needs as they arose. Her children hadn't reached the stage of being conscious of dress and insisting on special clothes. Lab School stressed simple limits and broad choices, such as wearing clothes for playing and shoes that protect the feet. No flip-flops or Sunday best! Parents helped each other in many ways.

The adults' use of language to communicate limits and choices was important for the parents' learning how to function during the school day. By using simple language, asking questions, expressing wants, ideas, and emotions, and making choices, parents and children all gained respect for one another, along with self-control and confidence in their roles.

Talking about problems during the parent classes enabled parents to gain a more objective view of their own child's overall development. All individuals were encouraged to contribute to these conversations. Each person's ideas were accepted and discussed. Trusting other adults for their child's safety was the result of these Lab School problem-solving activities. Problems were not ignored! Outcomes varied and decisions were made whether to make some change or not. Chapters that follow about physical, emotional/social, and cognitive development will give more information about the challenges that growing children and new parents experience. All learned from each other and developed closer bonds.

One's original physical and emotional family bond, trusting each other, is primary and always developing. Through this bond, humans develop a sense of connections that form an individual's perceptions of life and their role in living that life. Many parents developed a new sense of belonging, confidence, and optimism about their parenting within the Lab School group. With the protection of an emotional bond, we develop both respect for ourselves and respect for differences. The parent/child bond was a primary focus of parent education. It is commonly understood to be the most important relationship in every child's life. Not only did this relationship strengthen within each family, but serendipitously and reciprocally, bonds among parents, teachers, and parent educators flourished. Those close bonds continue for many as we contemplate the unique characteristics of Lab School.

How Parents Learned to Trust the Lab School
Building Confidence in the Program

A widely known Swiss psychologist, Jean Piaget (1896-1980), observed children's physical, social, emotional, and cognitive stages of development and theorized about the timing of specific skills that children develop as they grow through different stages. His name and theory were familiar to teachers and some parents. Piaget's observations and definitions of children's development have been expanded by other experts, including Arnold Gesell, M.D., psychologist, pediatrician, and professor. He worked in the Clinic of Child Development at Yale University, and his child development books (co-authored with Ilg and Ames) were readily available to parents. Both Piaget and Gesell described the predictable stages of development that supplied a way for medical personnel and teachers to assess children's development. Parents gained insight and understanding that children's behavior changes and grows in predictable ways. They also learned strategies for expanding the skills typical of the age and stage of their child.

As Lab School was just getting underway, Barbara Young learned Jean Piaget was scheduled as the keynote inaugural speaker for the 1971 opening of the University of Miami-Mailman Center for Child Development at the Miller School of Medicine. She invited the Parent Educator and Teacher from the new Lab School in Cocoa Beach to join her on the trip to Miami to learn from this renowned child development expert. His presence, an unassuming and genial manner, captivated the audience. He discussed what he termed the sensory-motor and pre-operational stages of development that are particularly important and pertinent to the ages of the Lab School children. His demeanor and ideas spellbound the audience. The newly hired Lab School faculty believed that they were on the right track.

In their first parent classes, parents were encouraged to be open to various solutions and behavior management practices, with the goal that children could ultimately manage their own behavior. The attributes described by Jean Piaget, Arnold Gesell, Erik Erikson, and Alexander Maslow defined age-appropriate expectations for parents and children that help define this goal. Parents gained a broad view of how families and individuals develop during their early childhood years.

As the Lab School program grew, other developmental information came from more contemporary researchers who were invited to speak at the college to the parents in lieu of the typical weekly night meeting. Their contributions will also be found in the following chapters as we describe the children's physical, emotional/social, and cognitive behaviors. The local newspaper, *Florida Today*, announced the lectures and invited the entire Brevard County community to attend. Lab School faculty and the parents were learning new research about brain and nervous system development, cognitive and emotional development, temperament styles and differences, and managing difficult behaviors and unique personality types.

Monthly in-service training for all faculty often reflected Barbara Young's personal curiosity about new discoveries in how humans learn and grow. All faculty gained innovative ideas and choices during these sessions. Barbara discussed current research and historical information about child development, and the faculty sought alternative solutions for problems arising in each school group. Barbara's enthusiasm for learning was infectious!

Often, the problems mentioned by a Parent Educator or Teacher overlapped with related questions from the other Lab Schools and served to encourage joint problem solving and creative solutions. More importantly, the educators bonded with a sense of commitment and enthusiasm about their work in Lab School. Feelings of competence, acceptance, and trust among the faculty, bolstered during these in-service sessions, carried over to the night meetings at their schools and ultimately, to the children. The parents came to embrace the innovative ideas that they were incorporating into their school and family life.

Barbara regularly met with parent reps from each school to share ideas and learn how different classrooms offered unique play opportunities. Together, they organized school-wide events like Family Fun Day, where families enjoyed activities such as obstacle courses, messy play, and water games. Parents also collaborated on projects like a Lab School recipe book, helping families connect and form lasting friendships.

To better understand children's development, Barbara created the Developmental Task Inventory (DTI), which outlined typical behavior sequences and growth in areas like movement, language, social, and thinking skills. The DTI was posted for parents to observe and track their children's progress during play, focusing on key areas like coordination, emotional and social development, perception, memory, and language.

How Parents Empowered Each Other at Lab School
Fostering Growth through Protection, Permission, and Shared Strength

Each parent understood the meaning of ideas about protection, permission, and power as they sought to manage their children's behavior. The children also began to develop some understanding of those concepts during their Lab School morning. Lab School protected children's individual needs for safety with the many adults present during the school day. The child enjoyed the permission to follow his or her interests and needs. All managed the power to make choices, communicate with others to nurture friendships, and adapt to change.

In most activities, adults did not direct children's activities but were present to observe, nurture, and ensure the safety of all. They responded to the children's choices, answering and asking questions, and adding information to expand the child's awareness of his or her skills. They developed patterns of communication beyond telling children what to do. They learned to respect differences in ideas, emotions, and needs, enhancing the human bond both physically and emotionally.

Both children and adults learned from each other when they needed to develop different strategies for entering an area where other children used a desired toy or equipment. Emotional and physical reactions and dialogue about disappointment, sadness, or outrage were acceptable subjects for discussion and problem solving. Often, the parents and children learned this at the same time. They also saw opportunities to put these rules into practice away from school. A child's initial uncertainty as they encountered new ways to play could ultimately and confidently transform into new energy to learn new skills.

Here are examples that reveal how parents learned to nurture the children as they adapted to Lab School environment and choices, and reacted to its rules and limits:

A simple question, "Where are you going to start playing today?" might invite the child's movement toward a chosen interest area. If the playground was one of the first activities available, a parent might ask, "Are you going to choose the swings or the jungle gym or the sandbox?" If the child communicated "swings" when all the swings were in use, the parent might suggest, "We could go ask Sam and Mary to tell you when they are through swinging so you could have a turn." The child could choose to wait or find something else to do until space was available. The parent would find the child who was waiting so that they could have their turn.

A child's uncertainty about separating and/or an attachment to a special blanket or toy might be offered a choice.

Charlie had a security blanket, an item which many children often use while adapting to new experiences. This relic from infancy or toddlerhood was understood as a familiar choice/process. Some parents even remembered one from their own childhood. The child was responsible for wrestling stability from the worn and trusted blanket to one's own bodily processes. "You are in charge of yourself at school, and you will be responsible for your blanket, too. You can decide." If the child insisted on bringing the blanket, the child's parent said it was the child's decision. He was responsible for caring for himself and the blanket while at school. These sobering thoughts might take a few minutes for the child to process; most often, the child asked his mother if she would take it and bring it back when she picked him up after school. Some parents recalled their own "lovey" from childhood and recognized the importance of this process in developing separation and independence in the child.

One father who had only attended parent night meetings had his first time at school on a Saturday Fathers' Day, when only dads or working parents came to school with their child. Her mother had followed some simple routines during the first months of Toddler class so that the child was able to communicate, largely non-verbally, with her father, on how to manage their time at school.

As they entered the art area, a father asked his daughter, "What are we supposed to do here?" She led him to the art supply shelves, chose some playdoh, and showed him where to sit, all non-verbally. He continued to ask questions and follow her lead: "What do we do with this? How did you do that? How can I make that?" While squeezing, pinching, and pounding the playdoh, lots of fine motor development was at play as he sat next to her, also using the playdough. She made some verbal responses as they continued their play and as he imitated her movements. As the child's interest seemed to wane, he asked, "What will we do next?" and the child moved to put the playdoh in its container and back on the shelf and went to her next choice, dad following her lead into the area where they did puzzles.

The child demonstrated that she had learned to do something she liked, to find it, use it, and put it back in its place for someone else to use. His cheerful invitation to her as the leader in a place where he was unfamiliar with specific plans and procedures was a topic of the next parent education class. She had a firm sense of self-control and knew how to plan and guide her father to do something new! He recognized his child's perspective and showed confidence in her functioning, reflecting his joy in her independence and competence. He seemed to enjoy imitating the role of the child! She was not yet three years old.

Conversations about social and emotional challenges often occurred among parents, who welcomed their contact with others facing similar changes in their life with children. They found the protection of the other parents, safety to express their own feelings, and the power to create a new image of themselves. Parent!

On another Father's Day at a different school, one dad arrived a bit late, "It's hard!!! Breakfast, getting her dressed..." as he apologized for his unshaven and late arrival. He explained that he wasn't used to the early morning routines and how his daughter missed predictable routines with her mother who had planned a weekend away with other Lab School's moms to coincide with Father's Day at school. This dad had a new appreciation for morning challenges. He heard support from other dads, all recognizing how all their lives were changing. In this parent group, many of the mothers were questioning whether they would resume careers they had left when their child was born, questioning the loss of family income. They had also become intrigued by their new role as mothers. As a group, these families, both mothers and fathers, had become important to each other in new ways. The mutual support of these families for one another, their bond, continues today, even in their children's adulthood.

Implementing the problem-solving process with children who don't seem to understand how to share requires parents to understand the complexity of the preschool child's physical, emotional, cognitive, and social development. A three-year-old child can walk, talk, independently eat, drink, and manipulate toys. "Sharing" is an abstract concept they will learn in time. The toys belonged to the school. The child using the toy was not required to give it up, to "share". When the child was through using the toy, that child was asked to tell a child waiting for it, that the toy was available.

However, each child's wide range of skills challenges parents' expectations as they join a group of preschool children. Taking the moments to work toward solutions for conflicts over using and sharing toys enables children to adapt to this ownership and sharing concept more quickly. In fact, children using a toy often give up that toy more easily when <u>not</u> required to "share." The process of a child waiting for the user to finish often appeared to ease the user's reluctance to share! The concept of time is elusive for young children. The suggestion to find the child who is waiting for another to finish using a desired object enriches the concepts of permission and power, developmental ideas for preschool children to learn. Parents were not "giving in" to children by not insisting they share a toy.

Differences in the development of individual children within a group were sometimes quite noticeable to the parents. Seeing the wide variety of developments produced concern among some parents at the beginning of the school year. Is my child too different? When consumed by the everyday challenges of parenting one child, appreciating the many differences in children of similar age was challenging for some parents.

After several weeks had passed at the beginning of the school year, a mother asked, "Is this a typical group of children?" The Parent Educator responded that, in fact, it was both typical and atypical. Only two quite active boys were part of the group of older toddler girls. The others were girls whose activity level included several typically active children and several quite inactive children. The parents and Parent Educator discussed characteristics of each child related to temperament and physical development. This parent's son, the most physically active child in the group, reveled in gross motor activity; she was concerned about him fitting into a group his age. She seemed to wonder if his behavior was a problem. The Parent Educator assured her it was not. The most inactive girls were engrossed in individual toys most of the time. The group's range of activity level and temperament was typical; the high and low activity degrees were perhaps a bit more extreme. Her highly active child had well-developed gross-motor coordination; the low-activity children's visual/fine motor preferences and abilities were clearly their assets. Further options for gross-motor play were created, including more time on the playground. A variety of different toys were supplied for fine-motor and perceptual activities.

The parents of these children came to know their child's temperament and choices and learned strategies for expanding each child's experiences. Noticing and valuing these differences, plus learning to build on each child's strengths, was a goal for all. Rarely would any problem encompass a single aspect of development. Parent Educators needed to bring a broad child development perspective to explore answers to the parents' questions.

No Lab School group was like any other Lab School group except in their embrace of learning at every stage of life. New research and analysis about the human body's capacity for learning became another way Lab School instructors and families provided new understanding of each person's individuality and our common humanity. Jane Healy, one of Lab School's guest speakers and author of <u>Endangered Minds: Why Our Children Don't Think,</u> wrote:

"Genes set the outlines of mental ability, but the way children use their brains determines how their intelligence is expressed. The experiences with which a child chooses to interact determine each brain's synaptic structure as well as the way it functions for different types of learning. If children change the way they use their brains, the synapses are rearranged accordingly. The more they are used in a certain pattern of response, the less flexible they appear to become.

Nature provides a schedule for neural maturation, and increasingly complex modes of thinking emerge from an internal competition for connections at each phase of mental growth. If a child is glued to an activity for several hours a day, connections for that specific activity will be built up, but something else might be diminished. Moreover, if certain skills remain unused during their early appearance in the brain's developmental stage, neural foundations may wither away in the wings of potentiality.

Severe deprivation can have dramatic effects on the young, malleable mind. Less extreme variations in experience have less predictable consequences. The value of excessive stimulation to enhance development is unproven and risky. External pressure designed to produce learning or intelligence violates the fundamental rule: A healthy brain is stimulated by actively interacting with what it finds challenging and interesting in its environment. The environments that we provide for children—the stimuli with which we encourage the use of a human mind—are the means at our command for shaping both their brains and our cultural future." [7]

---

[7] Healy, J. M. (1990). *Endangered Minds*. New York: Simon & Schuster, pp. 81-82.

The following chapters provide further information about the physical, emotional, social, cognitive, and language development that guided Lab School practices. The goal to move the children to new levels of skill in all these areas was viewed as preparation for their growing bodies and minds for the challenges ahead in later schooling. The challenges parents faced as their children grew were more complex as they adapted to their new setting in Lab School, a process that would be repeated many times as they nurtured their child's growth toward adulthood. The foundation that parents and other caregivers need to provide during children's preschool years has not dramatically changed; however, institutional support for all aspects of development may vary.

As Barbara Young approached retirement in the 1980s, information for parent education was gathered into eight modules on all child and parent development aspects. Our perspective in the world of 2025 has led us to focus again on the most timeless of that information. Contemporary culture and research continue to expand this knowledge.

The Relevance of Lab School Today
Examining Its Role and Impact in Modern Culture

The unique experience of the changes wrought by the COVID-19 pandemic has also invited a reexamination of old ideas. Perhaps the current choices available to our grandchildren and their children will pose much different challenges than those we faced in the late twentieth century. Perhaps added information about the developing child may encompass more detail about their mind and body. Our culture has already changed in dramatic ways. Examining different challenges may reveal more unimagined complexities. But perhaps the desired outcome of parenting efforts won't change radically. Parents will still want children to have the protection of a safe and healthy environment, the permission to grow to their full and individual potential, and the power to make positive choices while caring about and respecting others. The ability to meet and solve problems is timeless. We will be required to learn new ways to know the meaning and potential of cultural changes and to understand how an awareness of new science and research factors into our time-tested problem-solving process. The place to begin still might be in the human body's potential, the physical foundation for how we react to change. What do our children know, and what do they not know but need to know? How have the differences in everyday life influenced our society, including our own and our children's sensory perspectives?

The next chapter, Physical Development, includes more detailed information about the physical foundations for developing the emotional, social, cognitive, and language skills that evolve during early childhood. While all these aspects of a child's development occur simultaneously in many moments of a child's life, information for children's parents, as depicted in the following chapters, separates these three topics, focusing on the significant aspects of each. We recognize that any problem parents encounter at home or school needs to consider the developmental issues that seem to be the prime focus of any problem. There are limits in any stage of development, as well as the potential of the whole child to grow and learn. Development may be smooth and regular or occur in fits and starts. One can be optimistic and consider that the problem in the physical realm may also need social, emotional, and cognitive growth to catch up with the physical needs. Even adult problems are multi-faceted, with issues that overlap. Notice in the stories of actual Lab School moments that reveal the ways children are growing seems the main issue but may also give clues about the child's potential for learning.

"Play is the highest form of research."

Albert Einstein

Chapter 2 | Physical Development

"Children learn on their feet, not on their seat!"

Barbara Young

Parent awareness of each child's unique physical development
poses new challenges to their parenting role.

Understanding Physical Development
The Growth and Changes in the Body Over Time

Barbara Young often repeated the phrase *"Children learn on their feet, not on their seat!"* to alert all adults to question the idea that young children need to sit still and pay attention to learn whatever they are "supposed to" be learning. Children's physical movements during their earliest years prepare their bodies for more sedentary concentration during a later stage of development. Every human body is physically different, with systems that grow and change over a person's lifetime. Each body has strengths and limitations; genetics determines possibilities, and experiences nurture individuality. Brain development, reflexes, and sensory processes in the human body seek a sense of stability or balance so that all systems function for the whole body's benefit. This state is called homeostasis and describes adjustments the body makes as it grows and adjusts to changes. Physical development in a child's earliest years includes changes and growth in unseen ways when it occurs in the body's cells, organs, bones, joints, sensory receptors, central nervous system, and brain. Varying rates of growth, organization, movement, and reorganization become evident to observers.

Reflexes prime the baby's muscles and bones to move. The infant grows from a swaddled body to one that coordinates movements that we first see in rolling, creeping, and crawling. Sitting, walking, hopping, and jumping, catching and throwing will follow. Physical changes in the early years of a child's life seem dramatic; infants grow from an immobile and babbling baby to a child who walks and talks. Physical development follows a predictable sequence of acquiring gross motor and then fine motor movement skills in combination with the sensory systems that see, smell, and taste.

When the baby processes physical information, its internal sensory and neurological system and brain are busy with a variety of sensations, including pressure, pain, temperature, hearing, seeing, emotions, and digestion. Early movements are complex operations involving a variety of senses, all resulting from the central nervous system's processing and brain development. As the baby begins to move independently and purposefully, patterns are created, new patterns reflecting the uniqueness of each child's growing brain.

A child's physical or perceptual skills maturation may occur later or earlier than other children; many skills have predictable timetables that may differ in different cultures. Babies in a culture that uses papooses will learn to walk, depending on when the papoose is no longer in use. Children who are deaf may acquire language through a different cognitive pathway, perhaps tactile and visual senses along with sign language. Social and emotional factors within the child's environment may promote or discourage the child from reaching the potential of their body's physical growth and movements, and influence how their internal chemical processes develop within the central nervous system and brain.

As the infant's rapidly changing body seeks homeostasis, the child needs parents to recognize the changes from stable stages to less stable behaviors with growth spurts. The infant's body begins to automatically reorganize itself as it responds to nurturing that recognizes how efficiently the internal processes are functioning. Weary, sleep-deprived new moms and dads look forward to everyone sleeping through the night, another sign that their baby has physically grown to a degree of stability in its sleep-waking cycle. Everyone is becoming reorganized, and the household gains homeostasis!

The parents' job is unlike anything a new parent has experienced. Infants may respond differently at different times to the same stimulus; how helpful it would be if each baby came with specific instruction sheets based on its body's unique physiology! Genetics supplies possibilities, while experiences nurture opportunities that create individuality. Even identical twins have some differences in their physiology. When all systems are functioning for the benefit of the whole, the child thrives, and the body continues to grow.

Parents are stuck with the trial-and-error method when a baby is fussy or unresponsive. A parent who discovers that a baby's cry was the result of a diaper pin not securely closed feels both personal guilt but grateful the solution to the baby's cry was so simple; and they carefully confirm the pin is always safely closed. Parents change and infants change. Disposable diapers come with their own challenges! In the early days of Lab School, disposable diapers were just beginning to be available and were not as well engineered as they are today.

Empowering Growth through Education and Environment
Fostering Protection, Permission, and Power for a Child's Development

Observing a child's behavior is a key to becoming aware of each child's physical development, from the crawling stage to jumping rope. Postural stability, tactile processing, and motor planning are other ways to describe the process of children's physical maturation. Lab School offered a predictable environment for noting how the child's physical and sensory systems process choices. Each child physically approached and managed the school environment in his or her way, making choices by moving their bodies. The choices might be tantalizing or overwhelming. Infants were offered choices; they could sleep, watch other babies and the new adults, and play. They saw a place different from home. Parents were encouraged to note differences in the children's choices as evidence of their child's physical development as they observed and protected the safety of all. They were encouraged to bring their questions to the parent classes to discuss.

Many of the school's play activities reflect Arnold Gesell's ideas on child development. He found that children follow a predictable sequence of growth, moving through cycles of reorganization and new skills, but each child develops on their own timeline. Spontaneous play highlights these differences, as children show new abilities in their movement and physical development, with stages repeating roughly every six months but at varying ages for each child.

Barbara Young created the *Development Task Inventory (DTI)* to describe the many aspects of development. Reflecting Gesell's work, the DTI portrays a predictable sequence and wide timeframe of how physical motor skills may emerge; creeping or crawling are seen in the first year; walk, run, jump, climb in the second year; hop, balance on one foot in the third year; catch and bounce a ball, skip, balance on a walking beam, jump rope assisted or alone in the fourth year and beyond. The sequence of all skills and typical development time may be observed as "beginning, practicing, or predictable." One does not encourage a child to skip when just learning to walk or to think that a child is reading who anticipates a word in a story. Lab School nurtured the many experiences that are the foundation for higher-level skills. Physical development provides a significant foundation for all the other skills, including cognition.

Motor Skills as a Window to Individuality
Revealing Sensory Processing and Temperament

Differences in development may be based on genetic differences in central nervous system sensory processes, pathways that form a child's temperament, and environmental support for the child's choices. Some children quickly plunge into new activities; others take their time to attempt something new. Both types of initial response are predictable characteristics for individual children and even during adulthood. Even children in the same family may have very different and individualized timing of growth, temperament, and pattern of skill development, normal for each child's unique genetic profile.

Parents' expectations about their child's growth may reflect their own experience through developmental stages and how they compare themselves to their siblings or peers. When infants are born, everyone experiences change as a new family culture evolves; each member of the family has new needs and preferences. How will everyone grow and thrive together? Observations in real time became the habit for Lab School parents as they replaced old ideas about predicting a child's future.

Their child's daily movements and interactions during Lab school revealed to parents various ways to nurture body awareness, self-control, and self-esteem. A child's " difficult " behavior was acknowledged, discussed, and sensory options were explored. Physical growth spurts often reveal the tendency of an individual to become overloaded by sensations and to become disorganized, to lash out or withdraw from a new stimulus. The fight-or-flight physical responses during a child's difficult moments were opportunities for problem-solving for everyone. An impulsive responder, child or adult, may learn the benefits of taking more time to make a choice; a slower responder may learn to act more quickly. Either response becomes a clue to a child's awareness of safety, seeking protection (safety on a secure base), permission (choices of how to manage oneself), and power (to know and to be competent). Parents whose growing awareness of their child's physical response style were better able to nurture new relationships and new physical responses. This is a lifelong process of dealing with the nature of our physical body as it experiences the sensory world.

The Role of Sensory Integration in Behavior
Understanding How Sensory Processing Shapes Actions and Responses

"I act and by my actions learn who I am."[8]

Barbara Young introduced Lab School parents to sensory integration theory and how individuals differ through the innovative work of A. Jean Ayers, an Occupational Therapist and an Educational Psychologist, who wrote *Sensory Integration and the Child*.[9] Ayers described the child's sensory systems underlying a child's behavior. As the brain processes auditory (hearing), vestibular (gravity and movement), proprioception (muscles and joints), tactile (touch), and visual (seeing) sensations, clues to a child's individuality become evident. Parents were learning how to observe a child's physical responses to various sensory stimuli and note the efficiency of the sensory systems at play. Did their child jump in or watch and wait?

Ayers describes sensory integration as a continuing and dynamic process. The senses transmit information to the brain, which interprets and integrates information from different areas and sends that information to the maturing body. An individual's behaviors and abilities become evident. This dynamic process is lifelong.

Several local occupational therapists supported an understanding of Ayres' theory and practice by providing training for both Parent Educators and Teachers and even speaking to parent groups about Ayres' theories and practice. Occupational therapy addresses a child's sensory processing, which is evident through their daily activities, and seeks to activate systems that may create some difficulty for a child's response.

---

[8] Restak, R. (1991). *The Brain Has a Mind of Its Own*. New York: Three Rivers Press.
[9] Ayres, A. J. (1979). *Sensory Integration and the Child*. Los Angeles: Western Psychological Services.

The sensory system tells us what happens in the world; we see, hear, touch. The brain interprets this information. Brain activity is the processing of stimuli, consciously willed and automatic. An environment rich in sensory stimulation gives the physical body the information needed to thrive and survive. Ayers describes these sensory systems underlying a child's behavior.

- auditory (hearing)
- vestibular (gravity and movement)
- proprioception (muscles and joints)
- tactile (touch)
- visual (seeing)

These sensations give clues to a child's individuality. Parents learned how to observe physical responses to these sensory stimuli and note the efficiency of their child's various sensory systems during the play available at school. The children could experience new sensory experiences found in the many choices available including finger painting and clay or play-dough, managing the heights of climbing equipment, tolerating the noise of others, or any play which the child seems to both enjoy or avoid.

The Role of Temperament
Understanding How Temperament Shapes a Child's Unique Traits

Temperament theory was another idea Barbara Young introduced to Lab School. Both temperament styles and sensory integration define individual differences. As a child begins moving independently, parents notice how the child adapts to the environment and grows. The central nervous system includes the brain and sensory systems, the skeletal system, joints, muscles, and systems that process light and darkness, touch, movement, taste, and sound. An infant's brain grows dramatically in its first year as it processes sensory input from its environment. Does the child react easily, slowly, with difficulty, or a mix of all three? The child's behaviors rooted in the sensory systems tend to be labeled as their personality, temperament, or individual differences. Parents found this information offered clues about their own individuality and their child's. They gained a better sense of how they might both protect the child's awareness of his or her individuality and permission to offer how the child might adapt in different ways.

Psychiatrists Alexander Thomas, M.D., and his wife, Stella Chess, M.D., published their research in *Temperament and Development*[10] and *Know Your Child*.[11] They were curious as to why children who seemed to be developing in similar physical and cognitive ways display quite different personality and behavioral characteristics. They observed and interviewed a group of children from infancy into their twenties, and the data provided descriptions of their behaviors without any interpretation that presumed the meaning or value of the behavior.

Thomas and Chess' analysis described nine identifiable temperament characteristics of behavior that were noted when first observed and seemed to remain consistent over time[12]. The stimulus for the behavior might be a situation or a demand, simple or complex. They noted a child's first response to a new stimulus until a consistent, longer-term response was clear.

---

[10] Thomas, A., & Chess, S. (1977). *Temperament and Development*. New York: Brunner/Mazel, Inc. Publishers.
[11] Chess, S. (1978). *Know Your Child*. New York: Basic Books.
[12] Thomas, A., & Chess, S. (1977). *Temperament and Development* (p. 2). New York: Brunner/Mazel, Inc. Publishers.

These temperament behaviors included:

1. **Activity Level:** the motor component of each child's functioning and the proportion of active and inactive periods.

2. **Rhythmicity (regularity):** the predictability and/or unpredictability in time of any function, regular and irregular.

3. **Approach/Withdrawal**: a tendency toward initial withdrawal or reluctance from new or unfamiliar people, situations, or circumstances.

4. **Adaptability:** responses to a new or altered situation: the ease with which the responses are modified in desired directions.

5. **Sensory Threshold:** the behavioral reactions to sensations such as light, touch, temperature, and show a balance of sensitivity and tolerance of variation.

6. **Quality of Mood:** the amount of pleasant, joyful, and friendly behavior contrasted with unpleasant crying and unfriendly behavior.

7. **Threshold of Responsiveness:** the intensity level of emotional expression, the energy level of response, irrespective of its quality, direction, or mood, and the stimulation necessary to evoke a discernible response.

8. **Distractibility:** the ability to focus and ignore distractions that could interrupt ongoing behavior.

9. **Attention Span and Persistence:** These are related categories. Attention span concerns the length of time the child pursues a particular activity. Persistence refers to continuing an activity in the face of obstacles to its maintenance.

ASPECTS OF TEMPERAMENT

1. Activity level
2. Regularity in biological functioning (hunger, sleep, elimination)
3. Readiness to accept new people and situations
4. Adaptability to change
5. Sensitivity to noise, light, and other sensory stimuli
6. Mood (cheerfulness or unhappiness)
7. Intensity of responses
8. Distractibility
9. Persistence

Thomas, Chess, and Birch (1968)

As they analyzed their own data, Thomas and Chess defined four general temperament types: Easy, Slow to Warm, Difficult, and Mixed. The physical manifestation of these types is unique to the workings of an individual's body. Thomas and Chess also designated which of the nine behaviors seemed evident in each of the four temperament types. Some evidence of all four types may be observed as we describe actual Lab School moments.

Lab School's parent education discussions about sensory integration and temperament created parent confidence as they interacted with children and other parents during the morning sessions. As each parent became aware of their own temperament and sensory integration, they discovered that differences can be an asset in a family as well as in their parent role during Lab school. Parents with different temperaments may enable children to have their own special relationship as they bond with each parent. Without an understanding of temperament and sensory differences, strong emotions about differences may lead to unsafe actions and heated discussions between individuals, even differences in the their observations.

Goodness of fit exists more readily with mutual temperament and sensory systems in any two people, children, or adults. Differences may require more energy and understanding from the parent or adult. Lucky is the child with a parent, relative, or another adult who recognizes common temperament characteristics with a child; that adult may empathize more easily as they interact with that child. Understanding temperament concepts helped parents trust that other adults were available to meet each child's safety and physical growth needs. Individual differences provided children with a sense of safety. Children could observe other children whose physical development was more advanced and seek or respond to offers of help as they tried new ways to climb, jump, swing, hop, and skip.

Physical growth, sensory awareness, temperament, and goodness of fit were all at play in the examples of children's behavior we describe from Lab School days. Parent stress and concern for their child's physical safety, their protective instincts, were a frequent topic of parent education classes as the children's skills led to exploration and a need for parental presence and guidance. Many factors determine one's perceived threats to safety; while children need to experience a physical sense of safety, emotional safety is also significant for a child's ability to thrive. It begins with the parental power that recognizes a child's need for protection that grows to self-nurturing as the child learns to provide for its own safety. Using the words "safe" or "not safe" builds language, and ultimately self- knowledge, as a parent removes the child from a hazard and when a parent offers information about what is seen or heard that seems unsafe.

Insights from Lab School Classes
Revealing Sensory Integration and Temperament Theories

Nurses and parent educators encouraged discussions about the new experiences of pregnancy and childbirth and the unique and typical. All could note the changes in each infant from week to week, with some temperament characteristics beginning to be revealed along with new motor skills and social awareness. Some of the babies slept a part of the time in class, but when most of the children were awake, the group would play simple games like peek-a-boo and learn massage techniques. A concern about safety in parents of infants continues to be a parent's job well into the teenage years and beyond. Safety was the primary concern when Lab School Infant and Toddler classes were created. Space for the infants was often found in the church nursery. Sleeping babies could use cribs, the floor, or their mother's lap. The various centers could be adapted for infant and toddler play, as movement and other physical skills were developed.

The following activity, "Up, down, all around," introduced sensory integration to parents in the infant classes:

The infant's parent placed the infant on its back on her lap and thighs or on the floor, with the infant's head near her knees, feet toward her body, holding the baby's hands in her hands. Each mother sought eye contact with her child. Together, the mothers say the following:

"We go up"... (moving hands and arms toward baby's head, very slowly and gently, not forcing the movement, then go down to its side). "We go down..."

"We go all around"... (again very slowly moving hands and arms in a circular way both up and down, being careful not to force the movement)

"We go out..." (slowly moving arms away from the baby's body out to the side)

"We go in"... (moving hands toward the baby's chin)

"And tickle your chin" (keeping eye contact all the time, mother smiling and laughing!)

"We come forward... (continuing to hold the baby's hands and slowly and gently pull the baby's trunk off the lap, very gently, not letting the head flop back. With a very young infant whose head and neck are not

strong, the adult places hands under the baby's shoulders and head, moving the head and trunk very slowly).

"We go back… and we go side to side (still holding hands or supporting the trunk and neck, gently rolling the baby's body, returning his back to the floor).

"And then let's all go for a bicycle ride!" (holding baby's feet, alternating up and down, knees bending as in a bicycling motion). Excitement in mom's voice! Auditory, tactile, kinesthetic, vestibular, as well as a social, cognitive, and language experience - senses integrating in both mother and child!

When infants begin to crawl, new sensory integration and social experiences are evident.

Sammy, exploring with his new crawling skills, noticed Jimmy and his mother. She held him on her lap and Sammy crawled over toward Jimmy. Jimmy had a pacifier in his mouth. Jimmy's mother greeted Sammy who moved closer, recognizing Jimmy's newfound power to move his own body. Then Sammy reached for Jimmy's pacifier. "That's Jimmy's Binky," she said, protecting her child's use of his pacifier. And Sammy's mother, watching Sammy's movement, produced his own Binky and explained, "Here's your Binky, Sammy." Sammy had left his pacifier behind in his joy and permission to practice his newfound mobility. The mothers protected each child's ownership of their pacifiers. Both mothers appreciated Sammy's new sensorimotor skill and did not stop his interest in approaching the less mobile Jimmy. Both protected and identified their child's own Binky. The nurse educator had prepared the mothers during discussions about how the older children In Lab school, where all toys belonged to the school, "ownership" was given to the child using the toy. The child had the power to share it with another child. The mothers' power to protect their child from another child's germs was a priority!!

One older infant-toddler group started their year in a building that did not have a playground. All the children were walking and needed time and space to practice. Behind the building a large open grass area surrounded by heavy vegetation looked like a safe place for gross motor activity and practice for the new walkers. None of the children were running yet.

The Parent Educator suggested, "Let's go outside! Hold your child's hand when we go for a walk across the parking lot. When we get to the grass, let go of hands and see what your child chooses to do." Some children kept walking, ready to explore! Differences in temperament and sensory integration were clear. Some stayed close to mom and watched those who were walking before moving independently, evidence of the slow-to-warm temperament. Some plunged into action, some looked back to see if their mother was still present. The adults simply watched, waiting to see if any child wandered away from the group, ever aware of safety concerns. Some went beyond the other children; some came back to their mom but left again with encouragement to go ahead walking on the grass. None of the children approached the boundaries of heavy vegetation on the three sides of the grass. No toys were needed to entice the children to explore. Some looked for another child to walk alongside. Social contact!

After a time, some of the mothers walked away from the boundary to be nearer to the children; some stayed as a boundary line should any child return to the start of the grassy area and seek to leave the grass. The parents who joined the explorers found and pointed out tiny flowers of different colors in the grass as well as stones and sticks. Cognitive ideas and information: emotional sense of power and independence - sensory integration!

Parents grew to trust that the other adults at Lab School were available to meet their child's needs for safety and physical growth. One older child presented a pattern of behavior that parents, including her mother, found difficult to understand. Temperament issues may help explain the child's reactions.

A three-year-old girl created a morning ritual that was unvarying. She arrived at school holding her mother's hand (slow -to-warm?). She led her mother into the reading/music center where a record player was set out for music time. She let go of Mom's hand, went to the record player, placed a record on the turntable and turned it on. She then began to dance, mostly twirling her whole body (easy?). This repetitive behavior concerned the other parents and stumped the teacher's repertoire of possible interventions (persistent, difficult?) How might parents introduce other choices for this child? In a parent meeting discussion, the parents did not understand the unvarying routine and were fearful of interrupting the girl, lest an abrupt change might trigger a tantrum.

The Parent Educator, who happened to be Barbara Young, listened carefully and recommended that the record player be removed before the child's arrival, to see what she would do. When the child arrived, she went to where the record player had been, and she said with surprise," The record player is not here!" An adult replied, "Yes, you are right, and you are observant." (easy?) "What will I do?" the child asked. "Well, I don't know. Let's see what some of your choices are." The adult and child moved together to see other areas open for play. The child chose an activity and became happily involved.

Routines are important for many people, but sometimes changes are desired or required. This child depended upon the environment to structure her choices. When faced with adapting to the environment without the familiar record player, she was able to make the change. While she may have some degree of slow-to-warm and persistent characteristics, by reminding her of other choices with verbal exchanges of information, the adult helped her make the transition easier from home to school. The parents' concern about temper tantrums was heard and modified as they gained an appreciation for a new way to understand a child's point of view.

It is important to note that temperament theory seeks to understand behaviors with roots in the physical/sensory systems, not to label or make predictions about the whole child. Thomas and Chess' descriptions of temperament styles reflect attention and focus on the variety of sensory experiences available to a child. Lab School sought to provide a variety of sensory experiences that supplied easily seen reactions for parents to understand. They also learned how their child's individual choices and sensory processes might influence their interactions with other children. We found that language and social prompting could ease the difficulties the child's sensory system might present as they encounter new choices. It is important to note that awareness of these behavioral types can open up understanding in both parent and child of new ways to develop new skills and new strategies. Repetitive behaviors need to be understood for the value or benefit of the behavior to the child rather than being dismissed automatically as "difficult."

Even parents began to identify their own temperament and sensory systems. They recognized how differences between themselves, their spouses, and their own siblings might be the source of different relationships. We all noticed that a child's temperament and senses were adjusting to the new sensations in the school environment differently. The parents gained comfort, stopped worrying or relaxed as they recognized differences in children as a reflection of their children's unique sensory systems rather than a deficit in their abilities.

Two Lab School families with four-year-old boys lived in the same neighborhood, across the street from each other. The two boys' temperaments and activity levels could not have been more different, one busy, the other more subdued. Their four parents noted how their own child reflected his parents' own temperament styles and joked how lucky they were that they weren't sent home with the other family's child from the newborn nursery! Each family's culture was a good fit for their own child. The parents had remarkably similar values, educational backgrounds, and responsible but quite different jobs. The boys sometimes played together, and both were interested in a variety of toys and equipment, but each with his own style. One child often made a quick response that might seem impulsive; the other's lengthier response time may indicate a search for a more comfortable, safer, or more reflective reaction. Either response is an effort to protect the child in some way.

The parents of these two boys all worked successfully together in Lab School but in separate ways. There was no attempt by the parents to see the other child as having problems with either high or low activity levels or different reaction as they played, although both families encouraged their child toward safety during play that might develop skills beyond their child's first reaction or impulse.

Temperament and sensory characteristics may become more predictable as the child or parent gains an understanding of its own efforts to protect itself; a slow-to-warm child may learn about situations that require a quicker response, especially related to safety. Whether any child's temperament seems difficult to a parent may prompt that parent to examine their own ways of managing new options. Self-awareness and guidance enable both parents and children to adapt in diverse ways to changes in their environment.

In the 3–5-year-old classes, children who experienced problems during play frequently asked a nearby adult for assistance. Sensory integration and temperament along with information from an adult, the need for safety, and social connection might all be involved in a child's problem. Motor memory and motor planning were posing problems for Matthew as he found himself in a pickle. Emotions can play a significant role influencing physical behaviors. Accessing an adult for guidance rather than rescuing a frightened child was a frequent practice in Lab school.

A large old tractor tire had been buried upright, about a third of the tire in sand, exposing about two-thirds of the inner hole for children to crawl through, sit inside, or climb up to the top, using the thick tire treads as steps. Four-year-old Matthew climbed to the top, stood up and yelled, "Somebody help me. I need help!" A parent standing nearby walked over and asked, "What help do you need?" Matthew replied," I'm up here and I want to get down, but it's too high. I can't get down." The parent asked, "How far do you think it is?" "It's too far for me. I will hurt myself." The parent asked, "Have you seen others jump?" "Yes." "Did they get hurt?" "No." "You could crawl back down." "No, I want to jump." She replied, "I saw Sam jump and he then ran to the swings." This conversation went on a bit longer. The parent asked, "Do you think it would help if we counted to three and you jumped?" He said, "Okay." They both counted, and on three, Matthew leaped into the sand. He jumped up and looked at the parent, his eyes aglow with excitement. She asked, "Was it as scary as you thought it would be?". "No, it was fun!" His tactile, visual, and auditory processing had time to consider many aspects of his challenge. Matthew's visual-motor memory needed support with details of what he was experiencing that led to his fear

Another child, Michael, had climbed to the top of the jungle gym with a different problem about getting down. His motor planning was encouraged and developed with verbal and tactile input as he made the downward climb.

A Parent Educator noticed a child remaining in the jungle gym as the other children on the playground ran inside to wash their hands and find a place at the snack tables. Four-year-old Michael was quietly sitting on the top of the jungle gym, each hand tightly gripping the bar. "Michael!" she said, "it's time to go inside for a snack. What are you still doing up there?" "I can't get down," he answered. "Why not?" she asked. "I don't know how." "How did you get up there?" "I followed the others. Now I don't know how to get back down." He was frozen in place, fearful. He was inside the large jungle gym structure.

The adult said, "Let's try this. Where do you want to go?" He said, "Down there." Down there seemed to be a large unknown space. "Put your hand here," touching his hand and helping him position it on a bar. "Turn your body toward me," touching his trunk and watching as he turned to face the adult. "Put your foot here," continuing with tactile support for his hands and feet, verbal directions and close eye-contact. Slowly and successfully, he made his way down. He beamed with a sense of both relief and accomplishment.

His fear and caution had sought safety. Michael's external visual and tactile sensations seemed to provide too little information to navigate independently. He needed the time and suggestions from an adult, giving visual and tactile cues to help him process how to climb down. As parents became adept at seeing and understanding sensory processes and temperament, they recognized these sensory foundations for not only motor skill development, but also higher levels of social functioning and cognitive skills.

Sharing with parents that every child experiences safety and sensory input differently encourages empathy for each child's needs. Parents often notice differences between siblings right away—some children are more sensitive or react differently to sensory experiences. Children who learn to manage uncomfortable sensations build tolerance and adaptability. When older kids help plan their activities, they integrate their senses more efficiently. Physical growth, sensory integration, and temperament all develop together, helping children adapt and feel safe as they grow.

A toddler's ability to climb up and down from a sofa is a considerable physical achievement. However, the table next to the sofa may be the next obstacle to conquer. One family was frustrated when their child's expanding interest in climbing became focused on a heavy glass-topped coffee table next to the sofa. "Climb down" and "No standing on the table" were ignored by the child. The parents presented their concern during a parent meeting and received various recommendations: restrict the child's access to the room using a gate, offer alternative climbing opportunities, engage the child in other enjoyable activities, relocate the table within the house, administer appropriate consequences. The idea of punishing the child raised disagreements among parents who noted the child's developing skills. Other parents suggested the child was aware of his parents' disagreement about what to do and questioned whether they wanted that to happen. One of the child's parents felt strongly about not "giving in" but letting the child's interest run its course. The other parent noted the pleasure the parents had in choosing this particular coffee table for their home and didn't want to put it somewhere else in the house so that the child wouldn't be tempted to climb on it and jump down. The new physical development needs of the child were at odds with the social and emotional needs of the parents!

The discussion and ideas provided by the other parents supported the mother and father to develop a plan about the table that respected the needs of all family members and to provide interesting alternatives for climbing by visiting playgrounds, providing boxes and baskets to climb into and on top of, climbing in and out of the child's car seat independently. The Developmental Index (DTI) describes "jumps and hops" as the next physical movements after "climbs," suggesting new skills that might be offered to the proficient climber.

And sometimes the children's sensitivities give parents valuable clues about what needs to be done:

Two mothers recounted a similar experience with their young sons. Each boy wanted to take his shoes off in a place where the parents believed shoes were necessary. One was waiting for a parade to begin; the family had a curb to sit on where the parade was slowly making its way along its route. The other was at a shopping mall. The mothers' concerns about safety were not sympathetic to their boy's repeated requests. Each mother finally relented, and one found on one foot a raw blister that was surely painful. The other child's shoe held a large dead bug all Floridians do not want in their shoes or houses! Apologies to the boys from their mothers were heartfelt and brought on new efforts to expand the boys' vocabulary to better communicate their pain. "Hurt" was the issue! Both mothers gained trust in the boy's sensory responses.

Learning how to deal with a child's physical awareness, and a parent's own sensory system, is the key to a sense of comfort and well-being, to a sense of homeostasis within the family. Self-awareness of temperament can define work and play preferences and lead to an understanding of both positive and negative aspects of choices. Problems or deficits in sensory processing may be managed and/or be desensitized as one becomes aware of these personal preferences. Sensory input may need to be limited or remediated at times. Tactile responses to some fabrics are relatively easy to accommodate. The all-cotton t-shirts that dad insists on may cue mom to recognize the same tactile sensitivity in a child who doesn't like some of his own shirts that are not cotton. Some children can't stand the tag at the back of the neck of their t-shirts and some moms simply cut them off, an easy remedy. A Disney World trip may overwhelm some children's visual and auditory systems. Creating new high-sensory experiences in smaller doses might help prepare the child for such complex experiences. Sensory reactions may be even more influential or powerful under stress. All humans can be helped to manage stress through their sensory channels.

In some children, a lack of integration of sensations in the mouth may limit speech and language. Speech therapists may recommend simple, silly noise-making that exercises muscles and tactile sensations in the mouth and tongue; they often send children home with lollipops for that purpose as well. Eye specialists can detect visual processing deficits that may be corrected with eyeglasses. Work and play preferences can lead to an understanding of both positive and negative aspects of temperament preferences and sensory processing. Extremes of sensory processing difficulties may be managed and or be addressed by occupational therapists, physical therapists and speech therapists, hearing and vision specialists, and neurologists who detect and seek to ameliorate extreme differences and deficits in sensory processing. Pediatricians can be helpful in directing parents to specialists for further assessment and help.

Fostering Growth through Play
The Role of Obstacle Courses in Encouraging Development and Resilience

As Lab School's parents learned more about motor skill development, sensory integration, and temperament, they understood the value of opportunities for the physical, emotional, and cognitive development found in obstacle courses, different every day for the 3-5-year-old group and often including a balance beam. One of the schools was grateful for a grandparent who built a beautiful balance beam of maple wood with support for both 8-inch and 4-inch-wide beams. Children could begin to acquire the focusing skill needed to walk on the wider beam and graduate to the narrower. A bit of colored tape on the far end of the beam provided a visual cue to help their body focus on the goal of moving forward. Not only did the children gain physical skills, but they also learned that some skills require practice and patience. Walking the balance beam backward and other abilities were on display as the children made their way through the various stations. The children often cheered one another on as they confronted difficult challenges! Balance activities are to be found everywhere: children see curbs along streets as similar to the balance beam as well as other invitations to practice balancing, using lines painted on any surface or even a piece of lumber lying in the grass, a leftover from another project.

Several obstacles or objects that require a specific physical activity would be set up in a sequence such as jumping, hopping, balancing, crawling or rolling. The children were encouraged to move through the obstacles three times or more and sometimes rewarded with the award of a colorful sticker at the end. Children often helped create the obstacle course with carpet squares, boxes, or furniture. Why do obstacle courses? Many cognitive and fine motor tasks the children will experience in school will involve sequences to follow, a routine similar to the sequences of the obstacle courses. Some children breezed through the obstacles, carrying on conversations with their friends, some progressed slowly and carefully, planning each move. Some balked, looked confused and frightened. A parent was there to ask questions and suggest a way to make the next move or empathize with the emotions children expressed.

Barbara Young happened to be visiting a Lab School and observed a child doing the obstacle course.

A typically outgoing four-year-old boy crawled through a large mattress box by lying down on his belly. The box was part of an obstacle course to practice crawling, on hands and knees, on strips of carpet and bubble wrap, and in "commando style" with hands and feet used to propel the children lying flat on their tummy as they traveled through the slim mattress box. He positioned himself with elbows supporting his trunk and started to move ahead through the narrow opening. He pulled his left leg up and pushed, his right leg did not bend as he dragged it along. "Commando style" is not easy!

Barbara noticed the child used only one foot in the "commando style" crawl; his mother happened to be at school that day and Barbara described her son's crawl to her, asking if he had been born with a club foot. The mother reported that he was. He had undergone successful surgery and physical therapy. His walk was now smooth and coordinated. Barbara told the mother of her own experience with a child born with a club foot. She suggested that further therapy might be useful to strengthen the coordination and power of the foot he didn't seem to be using as he adjusted his body during the obstacle course. The child's interests as he grew up might be limited by the less efficient functioning of the affected foot and side of his body, especially in physical activities that involved speed and agility. Also, an obstacle course might be designed to supply added stimulation to the use of just one side of the body at a time.

The child's physical body reveals clues too important to overlook as parents seek to create a world of possibilities for their child. If they also strive to create a good fit between their child's physical being as well as the child's choices within a safe environment, their child will flourish. The child will have permission to learn both the physical potential of its own body and the world's many offerings and challenges as well as limits, making choices to satisfy its own body's needs at each succeeding stage of growth.

Another parent experienced a new awareness of her daughter's physical development.

In the parent class, a mother reported her daughter complained about back pain describing the following: four-year-old Natalie was sitting on a tall stool at the kitchen counter using crayons and paper while her mother cooked. After a while, the child said, "My back hurts!" much to her mother's surprise. She asked her Parent Educator for any suggestions about the child's comment. At the parent educator's in-service meeting the week before, the discussion topic explored how the environment may limit sensory-motor experiences; the focus of the topic was how Florida topography (few hills!) and one-story homes without stairs to climb might limit the development of back muscles. Underdeveloped back muscles might be due to fewer opportunities to climb.

This girl who noticed her back hurt after sitting for the time she spent coloring was not usually attracted to the gross motor use of playground climbing equipment, usually choosing less active play. Her mother gained a new perspective on the value of the jungle gym and overhead ladder. Upon hearing about the child's complaint and lack of hills and even stair steps to climb in Florida, many parents started to survey the landscape and discovered a fine hill on the college campus for both climbing and rolling downhill as well as using flattened cardboard boxes for "sleds." That area became a field trip for the children. One child's needs alerted the group to find new physical challenges for all. And all mothers encouraged this particular child's physical activity on the Lab School playground as well.

Motor planning and motor memory skills are the physical development skills that reveal what is happening in a child's brain when the body's reflexes become purposeful actions. When movements are planned and repeated, as when a child learns to swim or ride a two wheeled bike, the child develops motor memory. One seldom loses these skills during one's lifetime. Most adults have many skills related to motor memory: brushing your teeth, flipping a pancake, pumping a swing. Consider basketball players' success at learning to make three-point baskets or a toddler mastering the use of a spoon. Motor memory is valuable in many situations, including when using a keyboard and typing!

Creating opportunities for children to expand their physical skills is an important parent job. Adjusting to individual patterns of motor memory may be needed. Whether the child is self-motivated for learning or prompted by offerings in the environment, repeated physical activities may determine the degree of skill acquired. This gives one explanation why many skilled ice hockey players come from Northern latitudes and surfers come from Florida. Social, environmental, and even emotional influences are factors in a child's motor skill development. Beware, parents. Your child's choice of skills or hobbies to practice may not be in the same activities you loved during your childhood and adolescence! Listen to your child. Many systems in the body develop motor memories.

Obstacle courses typically included three or more physical challenges that included skills emerging during the preschool years as shown on the Developmental Task Inventory. Children may seem to have mastered a skill but without enough time spent on the sensory foundations of that skill. Including "crawling" challenges for children who had progressed to "hopping and skipping," invited the children to remember how to organize all parts of his or her body in a separate way. As they encountered a table, tunnel, or pillow that might need to be crawled under or over they were reinforcing skills already reached but putting their growing bodies through more difficult challenges. Walking on a 2"by 6' board in an obstacle course might be the result of similar but easier challenges of following a chalk line drawn on the sidewalk along with a wider balance beam elevated a few inches off the level of the previous obstacles. A cognitive assessment of the subtle tactile and visual changes needed between obstacles challenged the physical skills already attained.

Barbara's mantra, "Children learn on their feet, not on their seat!" reminds us of the essential role of movement in the life of a preschool child. Their pride and joy that comes with mastering a physical task, a choice that is concrete in their multi-sensory body and their world, can lead to complex feelings and thoughts. With physical and social maturation, children's experiences and social contacts expand their awareness of their moving body to nurture a foundation for the individual they will become.

As the child's physical skills emerge, sensory awareness, and individual temperament pose new challenges for parents as they nurture a child's capacities and adventures in the world beyond their family bond. The Lab School connections provided safe and challenging invitations for the children and their parents to grow and flourish.

Chapter 3 | Emotional and Social Development

"Children's emotions are both mentionable and manageable."

Fred Rogers, of "Mr. Roger's Neighborhood," spoke these words in 1969
as he testified before Congress seeking the support of government
financing of children's television programs.

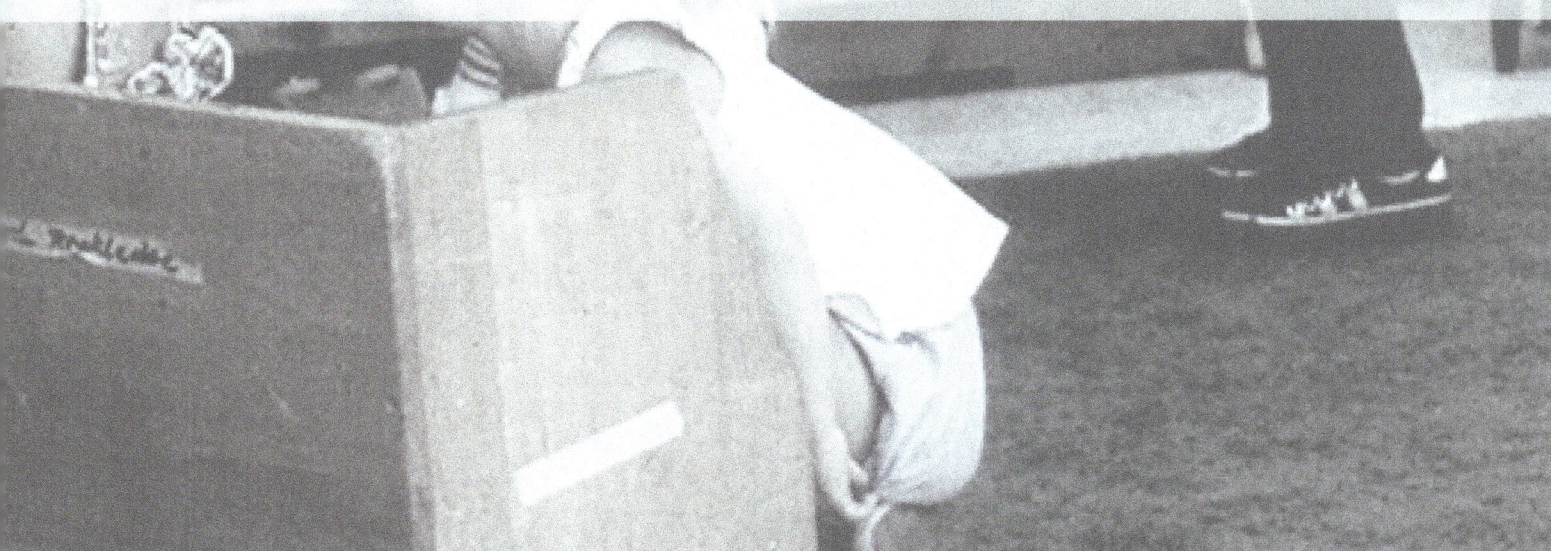

The Sensory System's Role in Development
How a Child's Innate Self-Protection Shapes Emotional and Social Growth

When a newborn infant makes the noise of its first cry as it responds to the sensory changes it is experiencing, as it comes from the safety of its mother's womb or perhaps from a doctor in the delivery room who elicits a cry with the physical sensation of a spank. The newborn's expression of sensory changes begins the process of the child learning to make noises as it responds to change. Sounds begin to express what we call emotions. The infant's social world and social responses are indelibly attached.

Physical behaviors and physical development are more visible, for they are seen in every movement of a child. Emotional behaviors and development are less obvious but represent a unique pathway to safety and protection, a predictable sequence for an individual's emotional and social expressions.

1. One recognizes how a body changes in response to a sensation or internal chemical processes; the child begins to have a memory of an emotion. Does it shut down or energize a response?
2. Is there a name or label for these signals? One considers either avoiding or reacting with a predictable response: yes, or no? Avoid or confront?
3. What are the ways to show this emotional reaction, verbally, act, or withdraw?

How will a child's sensory system interpret the behaviors of others, caregivers or parents, those who seek to provide for that child's needs? Will the child feel safe and secure or lost and fearful? Internal signals of emotions instantly alert the body to respond to sensory perceptions such as nurturing or threatening. If the alert triggers an outpouring of chemicals designed to protect the mother's body, breastfeeding may be painful and less successful. If the alert offers permission to the child to experience the milk, the feeding process may become more successful. This is an unending process unique to each person's sensory system. As parents become aware of their own emotions and reactions as well as a growing respect for the significance and meaning of the baby's sensory reaction, parents create strategies to support the role of these critical emotional reactions for survival within the infant's body. The process can evolve with feeding processes beyond breastfeeding. Bottles or pitcher-like devices can be used to feed babies when a mother's breast is not available.

An infant's emotions may be observed in its reactions to how the baby perceives offers of care: are the offers protective or threatening to the child? Satisfaction of hunger pangs and the provision of safety are the baby's earliest needs from its social environment. This dependence on parents and caregivers and the way the infant recognizes their attempt to provide nurture and safety that develop into lifelong patterns. Can a parent accept differences in the infant's response style and a parent's own sensory/emotional style?

This dependence and the way the infant perceives the parent's early steps to nurture develops into a lifelong pattern, a family bond. This family bond becomes a roadmap for the child's sense of safety; the parent recognizes and respects the baby's reactions. Parents who become skilled in recognizing bodily changes in themselves as well as in their child, give meaning to these differences and are able to engage their child to recognize their own internal messages and more predictably select appropriate choices that support its own sense of safety.

The auditory, visual, tactile, and physical movements being processed through the infant's eyes, ears, mouth, muscles, joints, and skin are sensations perceived by the child's sensory system, brain and central nervous system. The brain's limbic system sorts out and incorporates these sensations to areas of the brain for processing into physical, emotional, social, and cognitive responses. The way infants respond to these sensory perceptions begins the bonding within the family. Parents and caretakers who sense this bond change along with their child, noticing what seem to be their child's feelings of happiness and satisfaction, anger and pain, fear and withdrawal and sensory overload. Both parent and infant can begin to consider each other as predictable.

The infant's response is interpreted by the caregiver and the caregiver's response is interpreted by the infant. Physical and emotional safety can shape a sense of trust, empathy, and optimism, a warm and rich relationship when the needs of both parent and child are met. A fractured and harsh relationship results in mistrust and despair, perhaps generating aggression or apathy. The bond infants perceive grows from the perceptions of both parent and child.

Nurturing Emotional and Social Connections
How Bonding and Relationships Were Fostered in Lab School

A Lab School father, who happened to be an accountant, brought his three-year-old son to school one morning; his wife was at home with their newborn son. The Parent Educator asked how the family was adjusting after the birth of their second son, now several weeks old. The dad replied:

> *"It's exponential. Not just one more person in the household, but all these other new relationships among all our family members, including grandparents, uncles, aunts, cousins!"*

How succinctly this new dad summed up, with a mathematical term, the emotional and social complexity of the bonds within the immediate and extended human family! Emotional and social development and connections begin at birth, even prior to birth, shaped by each family's, each parent's, individual style, genetic programming, and early experiences. The parent/child bond creates a foundation for the growing infant's bonds within its family as well as the broader human society. The emotional safety of Lab School offered an opportunity for this dad to express his concerns and wishes, emotions both manageable and mentionable.

The body's internal sensory structures for awareness of touch, sound, taste, smell, sight, digestion, and heart rate are all involved as the child's complex sensory processing responds to its environment. Physical structures may be fully functional or not. Blindness, deafness, and other physical deficits may delay the full expression of a child's emotions and thoughts. Sensations from the environment pass through the brain's limbic system which perceives the sensations, sending them to different areas of the brain for processing. This sensory processing may have varying degrees of functionality, with the result that a parent's offerings of comfort may be both misunderstood or accepted and remembered by the baby. These first moments in the bonding process have a profound effect on the emotional and social development of the family.

Bonding actually may begin in utero; the environment influences infant behavior as the infant responds to social experiences. One mother reported sensing increased fetal activity during pregnancy in an environment with certain music or sound, recalling that the sounds at the Chuck-E-Cheese birthday parties produced predictable vigorous movements by her baby in utero. Another mother described a game she played with her infant in utero. When she pushed back on the tiny foot making a kick, the baby would withdraw, then kick again, seeming to expect a response. Socializing? A baby's first cry, first sounds seem to announce, "I'm Here!" bringing joy and relief to all who are in a delivery room. Obstetric care and hospital processes have changed over our lifetime to better enable parents and their infants to build a bond in the moments after birth. Their bond becomes more complex over time, a kind of equilibrium that evolves and changes based on each individual's internal sense of threats and needs.

The parents' bond with their original family and experiences of their childhood, as well as their infant's ability to respond to a parent's nurturing, have been described by Selma Fraiberg in the book[13] as the "Ghost in the Nursery," a growing and interwoven history of genetic and environmental influences in the bonding moments. From these memories, these "Ghosts" may become a significant factor, potentially positive or negative, in the parents' recognition of their bond with their child.

The quality of this process expands with the growing physical discrimination and awareness. How the parents and children communicate verbally and non-verbally can influence the trust the infant feels in its family. British psychologist John Bowlby described bonding as "a lasting psychological connectedness."[14] He was particularly interested in the anxiety and distress that children experience when separated from their parents.

A more contemporary researcher, Burton White, PhD, wrote *The First Three Years of Life* in 1967.[15] An authority on family bonding and the individual differences in all humans, White suggested that the quality of the family bond, both offered and perceived, may vary with each child in the family. Dr. White was the first guest speaker Barbara Young invited to Lab School's parent classes and the Brevard Community. He believed that children need the safety of their family bonds, spending most of their time cared for by their parents and other family members in an infant's earliest years. White's ideas conflicted with many women who were preparing for or in the workplace; he was a controversial voice. His book reported his research, which followed 300 children from their mother's pregnancy through second grade. He concluded that support for families during the earliest years of their children's lives was critical for children's success in language and cognitive development. Nurturing parents and family members who were the primary caregivers of their children, who read to and interacted with the children between 8 and 18 months of age, seemed especially significant.

---

[13] *Ghosts from the Nursery; Tracing the Roots of Violence,* Robin Karr-Morse and Meredith S. Wiley, 1997, Atlantic Monthly Press, New York, New York 1997
[14] *Attachment,* Basic Books/Tavistock Institute of Human Relations, 1968-1982

On hearing bonding information and Dr. White's ideas, Lab School's parents began to advocate adding Infant and Toddler Parent Education classes to the 3–5-year-old program. Lab School had gained further credibility and support from the parents! "Why wasn't this information available to us until the children were three years old?" the parents asked. The Infant and Toddler classes were added soon after.

Lab School added new bonds, new emotional and social experiences to the routines of each family. Many parents had already gained a sense of how their child was truly an individual in a world with other individuals. Just as the infant experiences a sense or feeling of safety in the sensations of its developing body, parents also experience a feeling of safety and success in supporting their child. Both parent and child can develop a safe relationship more easily as they navigate together new environments with expanding arrays of sensations.

They also saw a need for some experiences beyond the safety and protection of the family to help their children understand how to relate to others. Lab School created that connection between families. Parents took seriously their responsibility for children, their own and those of the other families, as they learned and practiced ways to communicate and solve social and emotional issues related to any problem that might evolve during the children's play. Trust emerged among parents that each child would be treated fairly and nurtured as an individual within the Lab School community.

Another author and bonding theorist, Ellen Galinsky, wrote in *The Six Stages of Parenting*[16]

"These bonding moments describe a family's attachment style. How parents perceive such moments may reveal a sense of security in his/her nurturing capacities of whether the parent develops a theme of control vs. lack of control as the child's communication and autonomy develop. They also reflect the lifelong experience of their own childhood and extended family, the unspoken memories within each family. They begin to reorganize their images as parents and as their infant reveals its needs and satisfaction as needs are being met, bonding with one another and in this process, form their on-going relationship.

---

[16] Reading MA: Addison Wesley Publishing Col, 1987

Emotional and Social Development in Early Childhood
Key Behavioral Stages Observed in Young Children

The typical emotions during the bonding process of children younger than two begin with general excitement at birth that differentiates into more specific emotions: distress into fear, disgust, and anger, and delight becomes elation and joy. These emotions are being mainly processed as a result of emotional interplay with a caregiver. The most decisive influence is facial, with tone of voice verifying the facial and tactile signals. The emotion and the intensity are a function of the individual's unique sensory processing system. Each parent begins to appreciate this unique system as they interact with their infant.

These stages of emotional and social development are evident in daily adult/child communication. The infant is displaying its bond with its family as it begins to withdraw from strangers; it withdraws from frustration as its needs are satisfied, and is open to having needs satisfied by other adults. The behaviors that change with maturation are a prime way for parents to know more about how their child's sensory systems are functioning, especially during the early weeks and months of a child's life.

Jean Piaget called this time in a child's life the sensorimotor stage of development. This first physiological stage of life encompasses the first months and years when the child's body seeks a balance of all bodily functions and achieves a degree of homeostasis. The family sleep-wake cycles become established, and the child's tactile, visual, and auditory cues are a guide for how a sense of safety and trust deepens. Homeostasis, regularity occurs within the family's daily routines. Automatic organization is seen in postural stability, motor planning, reflex maturation, gravitational security, and bilateral body use of eye/hand coordination.

What is the meaning of a baby's cry, its main avenue of communication, and seeking attention? Excitement and early interactions with parents begin with guesses, trial, and error. Is the cry due to hunger, wet diaper, pain, fatigue, overstimulation, lack of stimulation, or sensory overload? Parents begin to listen and observe the clues their child provides through bodily functions, translating what they see and hear through what is called "active listening." As they pay attention to what a child may communicate with some excitement, both distress and delight, they are respecting the child, giving it the permission and power to have its needs met through both verbal and non-verbal communication.

Every parent can attest to the challenge of identifying and meeting a baby's expectations and needs, and the parental joy that accompanies any success! A baby and their parents together create a family culture where all members' self-concept and self-esteem grow. Parents use their power to protect and nurture their child by providing a safe and predictable environment, allowing their child to use their growing abilities to express their needs and exercise their power.

Erik Erikson, PhD, describes this stage of human development as a time when taking initiative and having the autonomy to experience failure and guilt are at play. As both parent and child experience each other's joy, fear, and anger through their sensory channels of communication, a positive outcome can prepare them to try new strategies and communicate in new ways to set the stage for continuing to hope they will survive together. Is the infant experiencing a range of words, tones, gestures, and facial expressions communicating each other's senses? Are the parents getting enough sleep? Crying and colicky babies in distress may be a challenge for all in a family, especially as parents try strategies from rocking, car rides, and the noise of the clothes dryer that never seem to be but a temporary answer. Both distress and the growing autonomy afforded by physical maturation bring periods of relief to all in the child's realm.

Connecting Emotional Development and Temperament
Exploring the Relationship Between Social Growth and Temperament

In their studies of temperament, psychiatrists Thomas and Chess suggested that many children's sensory systems offer a clue to patterns in reactions that begin at birth and were similar throughout childhood and adolescence. These differences in behaviors are often called emotional reactions or responses. However, consideration of the child's overall temperament may be a more helpful way to understand and guide a child. Learning about these temperament differences in Lab School began with the awareness among Lab School's parents to begin to interpret their own sensory integration pattern which had influenced their own behavior during their childhood and into adulthood.

TEMPERAMENT TYPES

■ The Easy Child
■ The Difficult Child
■ The Slow-to-Warm Child

Thomas and Chess (1977)

Temperament remains quite predictable as children grow into adulthood. Thomas and Chess described these general patterns as easy, difficult, slow to warm, and mixed. As parents in Lab School became aware of how their own sensory patterns influenced their own behavior, they found some consistency between their childhood memories and their adult lives. As a result, they became more proficient in supporting their child's emotional reactions and redirecting their behaviors through providing alternative responses and behaviors, primarily through language and physical responses. An individual's temperament does not predict or limit all behaviors of an individual. Options that are available in a person's culture may also place limits or opportunities that also influence patterns of behavior. How one's body adjusts to changes may both expand or limit their temperament-related choices.

Parent classes often included exercises to promote awareness, management, and verbalization of the parents' thoughts, feelings, and experiences that describe temperament. Such moments were icebreakers to invite conversation and self-awareness. All enjoyed amusing and creative responses as parents poked fun at themselves; parents were always offered the option not to participate.

The Parent Educator asked, "If you were a dog, what breed would you be and why? Parents responded with their own physical and personality features that were both imaginary and observable.

"A poodle because I have excessively curly hair."

"A Labrador retriever because I'm always looking for something."

"A mixed breed because my parents were such different personalities."

"A Cocker Spaniel because everyone likes me."

"A Boxer because of our mutual digestive challenges!"

The Boxer took the prize for being most forthcoming! They all got the point!

Shaping Behavior and Emotional Growth at Lab School
Three Core Rules Promote Safety, Development, and Emotional Expression

The Lab School's problem-solving culture recognized both limits and opportunities for all ages, especially as older children shared their ideas. A child's behavior could reflect their temperament or be a response to new self-awareness—like being "slow to warm."

One child vigorously protested when her parents dropped her off at school with cries, clinging, wails of "No don't leave me. I want you to stay here!" She sat on the floor, crying. An adult approached her, squatting down to her level and said, "It's hard telling Mommy goodbye, isn't it." Child cried, "I don't want her to go." The adult responded, "It's probably hard for her too, but she knows you will be safe here. You can choose some fun things to do." Child says, "I don't want to do fun things. I want my Mommy." "Would you like to sit here and be sad?" asked the adult. The child responded, "Yes." The adult offered, "Come and find me in the Art area when you are ready to choose an activity." After a few minutes, the child came into the Art Room looking for an adult who helped the child choose some art materials to use.

When a child repeats behaviors of a temperament pattern that are not resolved as easily as in this incident, parent awareness of the child's sensory processing may need to expand. If the parent has experienced similar temperament patterns, they may be able to help their child manage its own temperament with strategies the parent has learned to manage behavior during any change.

The age and stage of an individual's development and temperament were a part of any problem-solving among children and adults; the goal of a mutually acceptable solution was always at the forefront. Children and adults often have different ideas about the sensations, thoughts, and feelings that arise when a problem arises.

One might doubt that our problem-solving approach was appropriate when very young children were in a moment of conflict, fear, or distress. Wouldn't it be easier to simply separate children in conflict or use a "time-out?" Who would ever have expected an older two-year-old to teach the adults in his toddler class about his sense of empathy for another young child? His ability to use words to explain his actions added to an awareness of his own growing sense of power.

A loud cry in a toddler class brought several parents and the Parent Educator to two boys, Mark and Robert. Robert was crying. "What happened?" the adult asked as she sat on the floor with the two boys. Robert said, "He hit me!" The adult asked, "Mark, did you hit him? Can you tell him why you hit him? Did you want to hurt him?" Mark nodded, yes, then was silent. "Tell him why you hit him." Mark finally said, "He pushed down my friend Jack" (another child in the class). "Are you hurt, Robert? Where?" she asked. Robert nodded, "Yes". Some comfort was offered, but no blood was evident, and he did not indicate where he was hurt, so the discussion continued. "Hitting hurts! Do you boys like to get hurt?" Mark and Robert both nodded," No." "Nobody likes to get hurt. What can we do when we feel mad at someone and want to hurt them? Silence. "Can you find a mom who might help you figure out what is going on, like we are doing now?" Both nodding, "yes," So the adult continued the discussion.

"Mark, why did you hit Robert?" "He pushed down my friend Jack (another child in the class) on the playground, and I didn't like that." "That is a problem," said the adult." So, you were mad at him for pushing Jack down and didn't want your friend Jack to get hurt?" Mark nodded, "Yes." Mark's empathy for Jack, pushed down by Robert, was surprising to hear from this boy who was not yet three years old. While it did not excuse Mark from further discussion about what to do when something happens that you don't like or that you feel angry about, the adult suggested, "A mom or teacher can help you solve any problem when you are mad at someone. Robert, why did you push Jack down?" Robert didn't respond. "It is important to talk about things you don't like and that you want to change. I'm sad when anyone gets hurt! Will you ask for help next time you feel angry, feel like hurting someone? Like we are doing now?" Both boys nodded, "Yes." Both responded quickly, the one who pushed and the one who hit, with impulsive behaviors. As they matured, learning to name and manage their feelings was a task for both. "Are you ready to go back to play?" The children nodded, "Yes." A parent said, "We need to use words and not hit others!" All the children and adults returned to their play. Hopefully, the children's language rather than physical acts would become the first choice for these young children in time.

Discussion about this incident in the next parent class gave parents new ideas about using names for feelings and ways to talk about feelings with their toddlers. A "time out" that isolates a child deemed an aggressor may not yield the desired emotional learning. Problem solving provided time for thoughts and emotions to be expressed. Everyone was learning.

Toddlers with limited verbal skills often communicate through physical actions. This shows parents how important their verbal responses are, like saying, "Ow! That hurts!" or "I don't like to get hurt!" when a child pulls hair or a beard.

Understanding Individual Differences in Development
Stanley Greenspan, M.D.'s Insights on Emotional and Social Growth

Author and theorist Stanley Greenspan, M.D., suggested in his book *First Feelings*[17] that an individual's genetics and experiences are key to understanding their development. His insights reflected many of the ideas already included in Lab School's parent education classes and offered some new definitions on the stages of development.

---

[17] Greenspan, S. I. (1985). *First Feelings: Milestones in the Emotional Development of Your Baby and Child*. New York: Penguin Books.

A video was also available depicting Greenspan's suggestion that relationships between adults and children include what he called "Floor Time," a practice adults can use to enhance communication with young children. Experiencing the "Floor Time" video gave Lab School's parents an opportunity to focus on the process, including the physical sensations, and reduce any threat the child might experience. The parents' response to the video was, "Well, haven't we been doing that all along?" Indeed, they had; Lab School adults moved to the child's eye level on a regular basis, always during problem-solving moments and often during their play! The parents had learned to respect and empathize with the child's level of understanding and physical sense of size.

> *An experiential activity in parent class gave parents a taste of a child's point of view during communication with an adult. Eye contact can be established with both parent and child standing, but the connection is more powerful with both at the same physical level as in "floor time."*
>
> *Two parents were asked to come to the center of the group, one standing and one sitting on the floor. They were asked to talk to each other about anything they wanted. After they exchanged three or four sentences, the parent educator asked them what it was like from each level, standing or sitting. The sitter complained how uncomfortable it was to have to look up all the time; her neck hurt. If a footstool or chair was available for one of the pair to stand upon, the neck of the sitting adult was even more stressed. The standing adult noted the sense of power over the sitting parent. Other volunteers tried the experiment and confirmed the discomfort of looking up at the adult standing. Individual differences!*
>
> *Perhaps the few moments the adult on the floor spent looking up may be indicative of muscles not accustomed to looking up as much as the muscles are asked to do in the child's neck. Parents were convinced that for an adult to move to the child's level it had distinct advantages and might ease communication. And there was a bit of well-deserved self-congratulation among the parents who had already recognized how much more readily children responded when parents made that adjustment.*

Greenspan also offered additions to the other theories of early childhood development milestones. He described six milestones of emotional growth and learning[18]:

---

[18] Greenspan, S. I. (1985). *First Feelings: Milestones in the Emotional Development of Your Baby and Child*. New York: Penguin Books, pp. 4-6.

1. Self-regulation and interest in the world (0-3 months)

2. Falling in love (2-7 months)

3. Developing intentional communication (3-10 months)

4. Emergence of an organized sense of self (9-18 months)

5. Creating emotional ideas (18-26 months)

6. Emotional thinking: the basis for fantasy, reality and self-esteem (20—48 months)

These stages reflect how parents learned to notice and understand physical, emotional, and social moments, the foundations of the child's thinking. They are useful to note in observations of adults as well. The earliest of Greenspan's two emotional stages, "Self-regulation and Interest in the World" and "Falling in Love," are evident in the infant/adult activity "Up, down, all around..." described earlier (Chapter 2, Physical pgs. 64-65). Before the child begins to crawl, to move independently, sensory stimulation through hearing, touch, eye contact, and movement occurs between parent and child, as well as the social and emotional moment. In Lab School, when the infants began to crawl, different interactions occurred between the children. As parents anticipated a child's interest in another person or a child's toy, they created an opportunity for both parent and child to begin a social relationship with another parent and child. Greenspan's stages 3 and 4, "Developing intentional communication and Emergence of an organized sense of self" can be seen when a crawling infant notices another infant using a pacifier in its mother's arms.

Sammy noticed Jimmy in his mother's lap and crawled over to explore, aware of his newfound power to explore! Jimmy had a pacifier in his mouth. Jimmy's mother initiated a social connection, making eye contact and saying "Hi" to Sammy as Sammy moved closer. Then he reached for Jimmy's pacifier. "That's Jimmy's Binky," she said. And Sammy's mother, watching Sammy's movement, produced his Binky and explained, "Here's your Binky, Sammy." Sammy had left his own pacifier behind in his joy to practice his newfound mobility and his awareness of the other mother and child.

Both mothers appreciated Sammy's sensorimotor skill, his ability to move, and they encouraged his social and emotional interest in approaching and connecting with the less mobile Jimmy. Sammy was exploring! Both mothers protected and identified their child's own Binky, an important safety concern as well as social awareness of ownership. The nurse educator had prepared the mothers during discussions about supporting children's choices by recognizing alternatives to the baby's physical powers to explore rather than labeling behavior as aggressive, lowering the stress levels of all. Lab School protected both children, fostering a sense of self; Sammy learned he was important, and powerful, a learner.

Recalling Father's Day for a Toddler Class when a father's understanding grew of how much emotional and social growth may occur in a child's earliest years. His confidence in his daughter's development (Greenspan's "Creating emotional ideas" and" Emotional thinking") by following her lead as they played in the art room with Play-Doh and responding to her directions during his first time at school all communicated nonverbally. Pretending to play the child's role is a new power parents can learn!

Reinforcing Rules in Lab School
Strategies for Encouraging Adherence During Daytime Classes

Many Lab School moments, when children had conflicting needs, presented issues when some parents expected some discipline, consequences or punishment. In parent classes, we explained that the root of the meaning of the word "discipline" is to "teach." The practice of problem solving, emotional and social as well as cognitive choices and processes, not only teaches children how to examine a variety of factors when conflict arises but also sought creative responses to the problems enmeshed in any emotional or social conflict. It is a timeless process for moments when different points of view collide.

Fight and confront to solve a problem? Avoid and run away from the problem? Either may be the first choice for some whose internal sensory processes are predictably followed by one pathway. Lab School sought neither but came to respect the sensory differences and suggested options. The use of communication with words and ideas to solve problems before acting upon differences was the common Lab School response. Examining a problem from differing points of view and reaching a mutually satisfying conclusion within our simple rules was Lab School's goal. When the infants began to crawl and walk, the mothers were in an even higher alert mode, for these crawling infants' sensorimotor systems might not include awareness of their less active classmate's needs or ability to move. Social connections became less stressful for the mothers, as parents modeled a positive reaction to another child's social overtures, enabling them to create different ways of nurturing both communication and socialization between their children.

The Block area was often the scene of conflicts arising due to differences in temperament among the children. Three and four-year-old play in the block area often called upon the supervising adult to assist in fostering cooperation. The Block area in all the Lab Schools was a large space with a variety of large and small wooden blocks. Boys and girls constructed forts, houses, towns, bridges, castles. No more than four or five children used the area at one time; one adult supervised the area. Some parents might choose to simply observe the play. Other parents joined in the conversations between children about the use of the blocks. Many clues about a child's social and cognitive development emerged as they built with the blocks.

Three four-year-old boys were busily constructing a fort when Paul told the parent assigned to the area that he wanted to join the others. "NO! NO!" the chorus of boys yelled. "We don't want him to play with us!" The adult asked, "What's the problem? There is room for one more." "NO! We don't want him to play with us! Not him. He will knock our fort over." Paul tended to be impulsive and had destroyed block structures before. The parent told Paul, "They don't want you to play with them because they are afraid you will knock over their fort." Paul responded, "But I want to play with them. I promise I will not knock it over." The builders were not convinced and remained opposed to Paul joining them.

The adult asked, "Can you think of something Paul could do that would be helpful?" After some discussion among the three, they reluctantly agreed that Paul could bring them the next block that they needed. The adult relayed this to Paul who nodded in agreement. "Which block do you want him to bring?" The trio named the block and the adult accompanied Paul as he chose the block and presented it to the builders. The adult stood close by and observed the four boys work on their fort.

Paul had promised not to knock the blocks over, but he immediately became excited and knocked some down, to more outcries of anger and indignation. Paul looked sheepish, "I didn't mean to." The adult said, "Sorry, guys, he got excited and knocked them over. Paul, perhaps you need to stay over here by yourself." He played alone for a while, watching the others carefully. After a while he asked, "Can I try again?" The adult relayed his request to the other boys, who said he could join them.

Cooperative building ended in a large "fort" with room for all to crouch down behind and "hide from the bad guys." The adult commented, "That's an impressive fort. Well done, fellas. Paul, congratulations on keeping your word and helping with this project!" When words replaced actions in the conflict, the children's needs were expressed. They negotiated a plan for how they could work together.

Another block play incident offered an example of children using the word "mad" to describe their emotion during a disruption in their play, leading to more words and thoughts about cooperating during play.

Loud noises of protest erupted from the Block Area. The parent in charge of this area went to the two boys who were complaining. Tommy said, "He hit me!" The parent said to Richard, "You may not hit him. That hurts! Tell him what you are upset about." Richard said, "He took the block that I was going to use. I'm mad about that and I hit him. I'm very mad."

The parent asked Tommy, "Did you hear that Richard is very mad at you?" Tommy replied, "Yes! And I'm mad at him. He's been hogging all the blocks, and I wanted one." The parent said, "Well, we have a problem here! Two people want the same block and two people are mad at each other. Can we find a way that both of you can use the blocks?"

Richard said, "He'll have to wait until I'm finished." The parent asked, "Are you using all the blocks?" Richard replied, "No, but I'm going to. I need them." The parent asked, "What are you building?" "I'm building a castle." The parent asked, "Would you consider asking Tommy if he wanted to help you build the castle?"

Richard asked, "Do you want to help me?" Tommy replied, "Can I build the bridge over the moat?" "Okay. That's a good idea."

The parent added, "You boys came up with a good idea. Let me know how it works out."

In this incident, the adult took a neutral position, accepting all angry feelings and helping the boys calm themselves down. They were able to facilitate language about emotions and ideas about cooperative social skills. The block area was an especially good space for active four-year-old boys to learn these important emotional and social development skills. With the adult in a neutral position to help the boys negotiate, the children developed trust that adults could provide help and empower them to meet their needs.

The Block Room also presented a challenge for the parents supervising the area at the end of the day. The teachers knew the value of using the different shapes to teach the children about size, shape, number, all cognitive ideas. Parents and children learned that the thinking involved in sorting the blocks invited an awareness of not just the characteristics of each block, but also an idea of the same and different. Some initially considered it an unpleasant job to methodically put the blocks in order on shelves. The chore became a moment when parents modeled the thinking skills the children were beginning to acquire about size, shapes, and numbers. A valuable cognitive teaching moment for all! A reminder of the ideas such as "dress-ups stay inside," or "we only have two easels," "you will be the next to get a turn," were enough. The children seemed to feel empowered to manage themselves.

The Impact of Labeling Temperament Types
Examining the Potential Issues with Categorizing Children

The limiting nature of labeling any personality or temperament trait or cognitive ability was an important Lab School discussion topic, especially regarding young children who have had both limited experiences and vocabulary. A label from parents might subtly limit a child's freedom to explore pretend play that might be a worthy challenge. A child's physical and emotional growth might alter their ability to learn how to do some desired skill or play some role in a new and different way than others.

Most families began to identify and compare their child's temperament behaviors with their own. Lab School valued giving permission to parents to encourage and support their child's choices by breaking down the hard parts into more manageable steps the child was able to understand. Even easy children might need support for their perceptions and choices.

The children joining the 3-5 group whose social experiences were limited or overwhelming might be labeled shy, with behaviors Thomas and Chess might define as "slow-to-warm". This child might wish to be physically attached by holding mom's hand or not moving very far away from her to play. The moms were assigned an area on their working day, so if the child was choosing to stay close to mom, the child quickly learned he or she was missing some other choices. This illustrates the slow to warm child who was given time and opportunity to manage the situation with protection, permission and power. Another example is a slow to warm child who liked the blanket he called his "lovey."

Many young slow-to-warm children use a "security blanket," a "lovey" or favorite toy when adapting to new experiences, a relic from infancy or toddler time. The adults understood the importance of this process, many remembering their own childhood favorites.

The idea that stability for the child from the worn and trusted blanket could be transferred to one's own body processes was a power given to the child. If a child insisted on bringing the blanket, the child's parent was advised to suggest that it was the child's decision. He or she was responsible for himself and for the blanket's care while at school. The child was in charge. These sobering thoughts took a few minutes to process and most often led to the child asking the mother if she would take it and bring it back at "pick-up" time.

Some children chose to keep their blanket/toy with them, and some decided to put it in their cubby hole for a time before leaving it in the car with their mother. The child's awareness of the play opportunities and support of the adults gradually led the child to take care of its blanket by putting it into the safety of the child's own cubby hole as a place for it when the child was playing with other children and school equipment. "Slow-to-warm" often includes tactile, visual, social and emotional ideas at play.

Slow-to-warm temperament describes the child who often simply needs time to process the sensory factors influencing that child's decision/choice. Every parent sought to avoid tantrums, often loud moments when a child might be experiencing sensory overload, too many conflicting issues and perhaps conflicting emotions about adjusting to or responding to an adult or parent request.

Ignoring a parental request may have a simpler cause, that the child is focused on what he or she is doing. Remaining focused on the task at hand and oblivious to other sensory stimuli is an important observation. This behavior does not necessarily mean a child's temperament is difficult!

Jenny is an example of a child's mixed temperament type, both easy, persistent, and slow-to-warm. A parent asked the Parent Educator for help. "I can't get Jenny to go to music!" Jenny was still in the art area and didn't respond when the parent told her the art room was closed, and the music group was available. This lack of any response was unusual for this child who was typically quite adaptable to changes.

The Parent Educator found that the girl was busily coloring with crayons. She said, "You are using lots of colors in your picture. Tell me about it." The child nodded, "yes," and verbally described some of the things she had drawn. The parent educator sat down at the table near the child and said, "Jenny, we are all starting music and the art area is closing. When you are finished with your picture, come join the group for music. You could also take the picture home and finish it there." Jenny looked up at the parent educator, a moment when she seemed more aware of her choices, put the crayons back in their box and back on the shelf, took her picture to her cubby hole, and joined the music time.

Jenny's persistent behavior, wanting to finish her drawing, and her memory of school processes were both cognitive issues and strengths. By seeking a connection and communicating with her, these characteristics both came into play. By taking the time to make a social connection, gaining her attention with eye contact and sitting next to her, the Parent Educator's message was heard and acted upon. She was typically quite focused on visual, fine motor, creative, social play; her persistence, sensory, and temperament behaviors were all at play. This child had many cognitive skills beyond her age level. Her ability to see a broad range of options and types of play enabled her to choose and develop how she used her body in all types of play.

A child with persistent and slow-to-warm behaviors regularly came late to school. His mother sought help from the parent educator to determine how to be on time for school.

A mother had difficulties preparing her son for school, dressing, and eating breakfast. The Parent Educator had noted that the child played independently when he finally arrived at school. He gradually joined and interacted with the other children. His physical skills were typical, and he played appropriately with various choices available, but he did not seem attached to any specific activities or other children. They reviewed the routine she had sought to follow, which didn't seem to work for her. Morning television, choices of clothing, and breakfast foods were all at play.

They discussed simplifying choices and the sequence of the process to shorten the time between waking and being ready for school. The Parent Educator noted that his late arrival sometimes limited his time on the playground; he seemed to like the playground's gross motor activity. The mother then remembered that he liked riding his tricycle, which was a more physical activity for him, while she finished eating breakfast. She encouraged him to replace television with riding his tricycle, a physical activity which helped the boy wake up his body to a greater variety of stimuli, and gradually they arrived at school on time, and he started to join all activities with the other children more readily. His slow-to-warm, gross motor, visual systems were guided and respected.

Another 4-year-old, Josh, presented opposite temperament qualities.

He moved quickly and deliberately through many of his choices. His rapid movements did not interfere with school routines or other children's play. A parent educator observed him approach a water table on the playground. That day, the water table was used as a container for bird seeds rather than water. The children used the bird seeds for tactile/sensory activities like pouring, filling containers, dumping out the seeds, counting, sorting, naming by size and type, etc. After jumping off the swing, Josh had run to the table, picked up a handful of seeds, and distributed them in an egg carton by quickly running his hand over the length of the carton. He returned the carton to the table and sped off to another activity. He was typically full of activity and energy!

The Parent Educator was curious about what he had done at the water table and discovered he had put just one of the tiniest seeds in each egg compartment. His fine motor skills were astonishing. His mother was at school that day, so the Parent Educator took the egg carton to her, telling her the sequence of Josh's behavior and his speedy work with the bird seeds. She wasn't surprised because she was used to his energy and motion. They found Josh and showed him what he had accomplished, noting the one-to-one correspondence of the seed in the egg compartment, adding a visual sense to how he had moved his arm, hand, and fingers. Unplanned, he became aware of this math concept learned from an activity with tactile and fine-motor skills, visual awareness, and science. Curiosity was this child's driving force! One might think his speedy movements were characteristics of a difficult temperament. However, his well-coordinated body did not interfere with or disrupt other children's play. However, it took him some time to learn you don't have to slam a door to close it! Experimenting with different ways to close a door, quickly or slowly, might also add vocabulary and other cognitive ideas.

Enhancing Social Development in the Five-Day Program
Emotional, Social, and Cognitive Growth through Planning Activities

Four and five-year-old children make choices, especially around gross-motor and pretend play, and many have learned to test the perceived social limits. They may seem aggressive or possessive as they learn how to safely use their many physical powers constructively. Their questions and exploration must be answered without being diminished as careless or thoughtless, or to invite guilt. Greenspan described this as a time for developing "Emotional Thinking: the basis for fantasy, reality, and self-esteem." The "Power" meeting and "Little Red Riding Hood" in the next chapter will provide examples of this complex thinking, where children are acting out dramas meaningful in their play.

When Lab School expanded its schedule to include two additional days for the older children, their parents took turns with added workdays to keep the ratio of one adult for every 4 or 5 children. Since Toddlers also used the school building on those days, the Teacher planned when each group might use the different interest areas. The five-day group might be as many as ten 4-year-olds. They would often discuss a group project with the Teacher, identifying the necessary steps, deciding who would do particular tasks, and identifying different characters or roles to play. Enjoying the finished product was of paramount importance. The realization that all materials had to be returned to their original condition at the end of the morning brought groans and moans as they were dismantling and tidying! A sense of satisfaction and accomplishment prevailed.

The older children were ready for cooperative group activities like cooking, building, and projects that required planning, organizing who would do specific tasks, pretending to play a particular character, and deciding where the project would be located. We might use the playground to construct a town, design a house, a church, a store, and a road. Material used in obstacle courses included some of the boards and boxes used in the construction. Role-playing and imagination became important parts of the play.

Cooking snacks like muffins or grilled cheese was a reward. Some activities targeted skills from the Developmental Task Inventory (DTI). The expanded, more structured schedule allowed older children to build language, emotional awareness, cooperation, and social skills, while imaginative play encouraged creative use of materials.

The Power of Language and Cognition in Development
Enhancing Growth through Communication and Knowledge

Expressing emotions changes with age. Pre-verbal children show feelings through cries and actions—these are their first "words" for emotions. Toddlers often imitate parents by shaking their heads or saying "no." Children use words to share frustrations and feelings as language develops, and parents learn to support and expand their child's emotional vocabulary.

Lab School suggested words for emotions parents might use that were quite simple: mad or angry, scared or afraid, sad, and happy; "mine" becomes another powerful word. While these simple emotions will evolve with more elaborate or precise language as they grow, using simple, easy-to-pronounce words becomes more useful for preschoolers. While parents might not like to hear their child say they are mad about something, they need to congratulate themselves for helping them verbally rather than physically express anger. Most problem-solving moments include words for the emotions a child or adult might feel.

Children express emotions through language gradually, influenced by age and family use of emotion words. Emotions start as physical excitement, then become distress or delight in infancy. By six months, fear and anger appear; jealousy shows up around eighteen months. As children grow, emotions like affection and joy develop. Early smiles and laughs strengthen the parent-child bond. Simple phrases like "I'm afraid when..." or "I'm mad when..." help children learn to express feelings and solve problems as their language skills grow.

Childhood begins a lifelong process of understanding and labeling emotions while learning social limits and rules appropriate for each developmental stage. Children first find healthy ways to meet their social and emotional needs within their family's boundaries. If the family culture recognizes the challenges described by Maslow and Erikson, and parents are aware of both limitations and potential at each stage, a child can develop within the boundaries of their physical maturation. With parents providing the right level of protection and safety, children are free to expand their awareness and curiosity about the world. Just as a deaf child may learn sign language or a child may need glasses, naming and thinking about emotions follow a similar process.

Experiencing the Value of Sharing
How Lab School Children Learned and Practiced the Concept of Sharing

Every parent was concerned about teaching children to share. One way to consider this issue was to discuss the things they were *unwilling* to share; parents were surprised at how few things were in that category for themselves, and all the experiences it took to reach their current stage! Marriage and parenthood bring a different meaning of the word "mine," an important part of the sharing process. Are parents willing to share their popcorn or cookie if their child reaches for it? One might say, "No, I don't want to share, but we can find a cookie for you or make you a bowl of popcorn." This conversation between parent and child can begin the child's cognitive process at a level a child is able to understand. For an adult to command a child to share, when the adult means you must give it up, does not instruct the child about the process. The human joy of participating with others in a mutually beneficial project begins with recognizing the mutual feelings that can accompany sharing. Even a young child can begin to recognize that sharing is giving, which builds relationships! They will happily eat the cookie you are willing to share with them but may not readily share their cookie with you! Not yet. Talk about it.

Asking a child to identify toys that are theirs that they are not willing to share can take some of the social pressure off new relationships with other children. Toys that belong to a child that they do not want to share can be put away when a friend comes to play. The toys and equipment at school were owned by the school, available for the child's ownership while the child was using the object. A child on a swing might not be willing to give it up to another child who wants to swing; a problem to solve. The ability to use a toy or a swing as long as desired nurtured self-control. You could "own" it while you are using it! And you could turn it over to another child when you were through using it. Power! Parents were amazed that power struggles over the use of toys and equipment were nipped in the bud. Children's attention span was respected, and they often shared a toy when they realized they didn't have to give it up!

A child in Lab School who was using a toy or equipment could claim "ownership" of what he or she was using. Adults might point out that another child was waiting to use the item "when you are through using it." When a child said, "Mine!" to avoid giving a toy up to another child, an adult might remind them that all the toys and equipment belonged to the school, we were just using it in our time at school, unlike their toys at home. Adults reminded children that the child using the toy could decide when to give it to the person who was waiting to use it. It was remarkable that children often finished using a toy or the equipment more rapidly when they had permission to keep using it rather than give it up to another, a glimpse at a new power the child was learning. Adults also might ask a question that would suggest ways two children might play together. "Keep holding the teddy bear, Julie, and perhaps Marie will bring a doll, and you both can feed them a snack."

The children shared their parents with others at Lab School, especially as they learned their ability to make their own choices at school. The connection between separating from their parents and independently choosing their own way to play seemed to show both their secure bond as well as their curiosity about the new choices available.

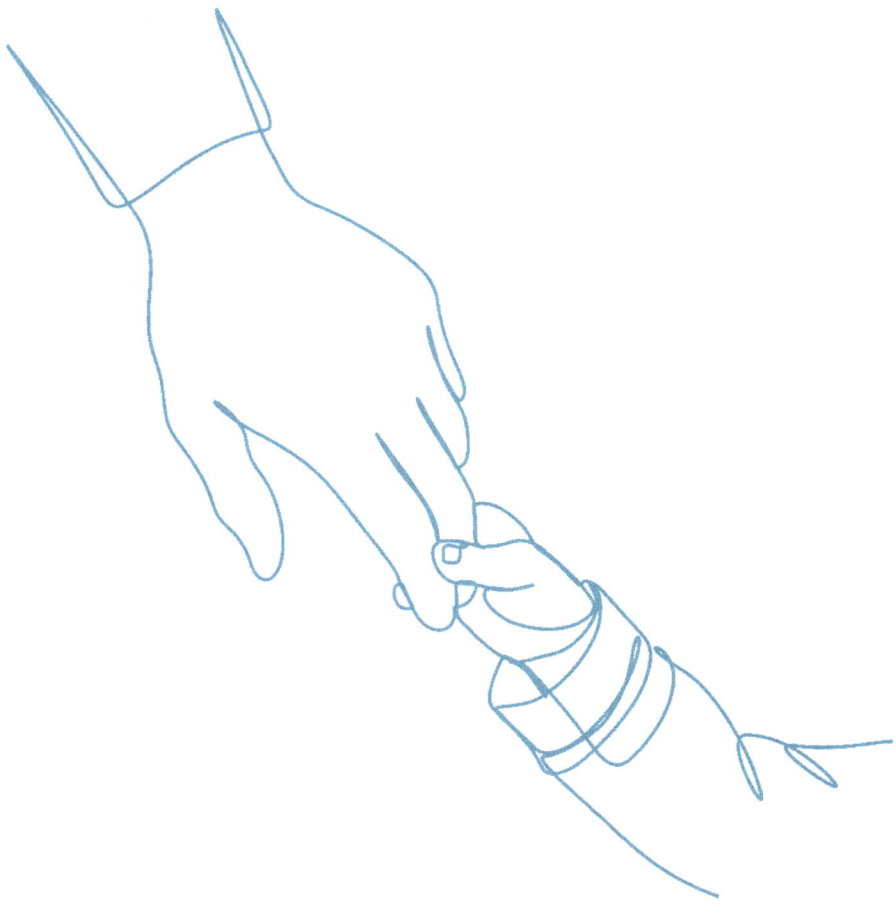

Reinforcing Social and Emotional Concepts through Media
The Role of Various Media in Supporting Emotional and Social Learning

Television, stories and books are prime sources for parents to expand their family's culture with language related to social and emotional learning. Even one of the first books parents choose for their baby, *Pat the Bunny*, can teach an alternative way to explore with a sense of touch! Saying "Pat, pat" while moving an infant's hand as the child grabs and pulls mom's hair can modulate a child's efforts to gain a parent's attention, a social skill. Oscar the Grouch is a fine role model for learning words and tones to express anger; everyone enjoys pretending to be Oscar! The parents of older children did not particularly appreciate the lessons of the Power Rangers! Creative teaching used the show's ideas with a lesson on how to use power.

Children's television in the early days of Lab School was limited compared to 2024's offerings. However, the emotional and social content of the stories and drama on both *Sesame Street* and *Mr. Roger's Neighborhood* gave parents another medium for children to learn about social acceptance and emotional needs. Parents often revealed an awareness of their own sensory preferences as they indicated which show they liked best. Not surprisingly, slow-to-warm parent types often preferred the slower pace of *Mr. Rogers*; parents who liked higher sensory levels might prefer the faster-moving *Sesame Street*. The language and the emotions of the characters reflected what we were teaching the parents, as did the *Sesame Street* characters and the neighborhood of *Mr. Rogers*. Pretend play was a vehicle for language to help children know and understand feelings and differences, all cognitive powers.

A whole new challenge came to Lab School children entering kindergarten classes. Twenty or more children with only one teacher and perhaps an aide created a new sharing experience. Parents reported that their children were often surprised at how different the "big school" could be. They shared the teacher's attention with many other children and the adults were not as readily available to solve problems as they were accustomed to in Lab School. And they had to do the same thing with the whole group most of the time; not as many choices were offered. For many, any conflicts they experienced with other children and with the large group activities was a challenge they came to resolve by themselves, sometimes with a little coaching from their parents. We didn't hear complaints from parents or kindergarten teachers about the Lab School graduates' social non-compliance. Children were used to their parents and other adults listening to their questions and complaints; they also had many experiences in figuring out how to adapt or make changes.

One mother told of the following incident, reported by her son's teacher, about his behavior in her kindergarten classroom:

> *A kindergarten teacher was teaching a lesson about the senses: touch, vision, hearing, smell, and taste. The former Lab School child in her class raised his hand and asked a question: "Haven't you forgotten one?" She responded, "I don't think so." He suggested, "Well, what about the sense of humor?" He was genuinely curious. Humor was a particular favorite sensibility for this child; he was quite serious about the matter! Luckily, his teacher had that sense as well, and appreciated his insight/question and could laugh with him. His honest inquiry and her willingness to respond to him in a positive way, as well as when she reported his question to his mother, gave his parent confidence that her son and his teacher were navigating his kindergarten experience in a positive way.*

Lab School children grew in cognitive skills based on their level of physical, emotional, and social development. Their skills were driven by their choices; if they liked the Art Area best, they found growing ways to use a particular medium in ever-expanding ways. The initial two or three-block towers by toddlers might expand into castles and moats that required more precise fine motor skills and cooperative efforts. The playground brought new competencies to light. The conversations between children and adults set a tone of mutual respect and cooperation among all involved in the Lab School. The children learned that adults were their compatriots in the grown-up world, resources as well as protectors. Relationships were a source of new ideas and choices.

The following chapter, Cognition, describes the cognitive development offered to children at every age as the result of the physical, emotional, and social support from the variety of caring adults they experienced during their Lab School experience.

"The brain's uniqueness stems from the fact that nowhere in the known universe is there anything even remotely resembling it...."

Richard Restak

Chapter 4 | Cognition

"There is nothing either good or bad but thinking makes it so..."

William Shakespeare wrote these words for Hamlet,
the character who did not want to be involved in a heated debate between
two other characters discussing the war in Denmark.

Understanding Cognition
The Power of Thinking: Pondering, Planning, and Remembering

Perception, interpretation, memory, and knowledge are all brain processes. The human brain stores memories, and we can think about ourselves, how and what we think, and why we behave as we do. Cognition enables children to gain an awareness or sense of the meaning of safety as they express their needs and ideas. Each of our human brains grows unique thinking skills with time and experience, changing throughout every person's lifetime.

Cognition results from how an individual's brain and nervous system grow and process human experiences. The brain also matures and becomes more complex during the different stages of human development. Memory and sensing and responding to one's environment build thinking, creativity, reading, and calculating with numbers, all cognitive processes.

Parents have many questions and concerns about what young children need to learn, think about, and know. Bonding is perhaps the most significant contributor to cognitive growth during preschool. Children depend on human contact during infancy and their earliest years, especially through their familial bond.

How the brain thinks and manages or directs behavior is fundamental to cognitive growth. In the Physical chapter, we noted how unique behavioral response patterns in the child's brain become evident in physical, emotional, and social behaviors. As their bodies and brains mature, children react to sensory stimuli, including reflexes and body movements.

Research continues to reveal changes and new powers in the human brain. That is, in response to any new stimulus, the first response may be NO (to avoid), or YES (to accept and see what comes next). For one child, a mere whiff of Aunt Sarah's perfume may be offensive or overstimulating, producing cries and pushing away or withdrawal from her; to another child, the same odor may be pleasing, producing curiosity and connections. Our perceptions or interpretations of sensory data become our views, opinions, and motivations, largely directing our behaviors and may become our cognitive style. As Shakespeare said, "thinking makes it so."

The senses begin a process that builds short-term and long-term memories in the brain's unique structures. We store memories about size, sequences, numbers, and differences in things we hear, see, touch, and name. We can think about both how we think and why we behave as we do. Emotions and a sense of safety are critical factors in understanding what children will learn from their sensory experiences.

Lab School parents realized their own sensory or thinking styles could shape their parenting. They began to reflect: "How am I responding to my child's cry? Am I offering comfort, words, or touch? Am I ignoring it?" Every response by parent or child has meaning and is part of ongoing learning. Everyone processes and remembers information differently, with unique timing and style. As children interact with parents and others, they gradually become more aware of themselves and develop new ways of understanding.

Richard Restack, a neuropsychiatrist, describes how the different parts of the brain connect and reveal cognitive functioning.

> *"Aspects of thinking like self-awareness, memory and logical inference communicate within the association areas of the brain. On one level, the brain is a localized organ with parts concerned with vision, hearing, touch, and so on. But at the same time, the brain resists our attempts to impose a geography upon it...if one part of the brain is damaged, the resulting loss of a specific function, another brain area may take over and make possible a complete or partial restoration of that function...neither walking nor speaking is a modular activity. Speaking is entwined with logic, abstraction, memory, and learning. Walking involves complicated alliances with the sensory and cerebellar systems. Both speaking and walking can go awry; therefore, depending upon where in the brain the damage occurs...whether a particular brain cell fires depends to a large extent upon the influence of the many other cells that contact it."[19]*

To oversimplify, a human becomes an individual through a continual process of receiving and interpreting sensory information as the brain learns to use this information from his or her environment. An amazing process! The goal was to align a parent's expectations with the clues their child's behavior offered! Even more astounding is that each brain is unique, yet similar. We all depend upon the same "ingredients", data from the outside processed by the unique body and brain each of us is born with. Our brains are, indeed, remarkably complex, the source of some of humanity's most fascinating discoveries.

---

[19] Restack, p 253-7, *The Mind, Simon and Schuster*, 1990. Restack Richard, M.D., born 1942. Georgetown Medical School neuropsychiatrist.

Building on Piaget's Legacy
Cognitive Development Theorists Expanded Insights into Early Childhood Growth

In the early twentieth century, when psychologist Jean Piaget first observed young children, he named cognitive stages we observed in Lab School classes: the Sensory-Motor Stage for ages birth to three encompassed the ages in the infant and toddler classes; the Pre-operational Stage described the children in the three to five-year-old class. He named the types and sequence of behaviors he observed that seemed most significant for development in each of these early stages. He also suggested that children who fully experience the typical behaviors of each stage become better prepared for the next stage. Physical, emotional, social, and cognitive development coincide. Piaget's theories have withstood the test of time as contemporary thinkers and educators have added ideas suggested by contemporary neuroscientists.

Lab School Parents began to understand the complexity of human learning in a child's earliest years, for all aspects of the child's body are at play at every moment. Growth is revealed as individuals interact with their environment; every child's environment is different, even if they are in the same family. At times during a child's day, one type of development may be of primary significance, as in a playground activity where physical skills of memory and coordination evolve or in a time when a child is exploring in his or her home. Emotional and social support may be offered to a child seeking new ways to use the opportunities for play with supportive language and gestures. Cognitive memories of physical skills grow into a foundation for new ways to play on or use different equipment.

Physical, emotional, social, and cognitive development occur simultaneously. Parents begin to perceive the complexity of learning, for all aspects of the child's body are at play at every moment. Growth is revealed as individuals interact with their environment, the brain changes with each interaction over an individual's lifetime. Every child's body is different, even if they are in the same family. At times during a child's day, one type of development may be of primary significance, as in a playground activity where physical skills of memory and coordination evolve or in a time when a child is exploring in his or her home.

One everyday challenge Lab School's parents discussed during the school day as well in the parent class involved when their child became aware of their power to use the remote control for the family television set. The parents learned new strategies for dealing with a problem as they became aware of the Lab School problem-solving approach and the value of learning from other parents who reported a variety of strategies to meet this new parenting challenge! In 2024, the remote-control problem has been replaced by the cell phone's presence, challenging parents to create plans for how their family, both adults and children of all ages, are using the phones.

Lab School offered emotional and social support for parents, encouraging children as they explored new ways to use the school equipment and toys. Parents learned to manage problems with supportive language and gestures. Cognitive memories of physical skills grew into a foundation for new ways to play on or use different equipment.

Piaget suggested that children who fully experience the typical behaviors of each stage become better prepared for the next stage. Physical, emotional, social, and cognitive development occur simultaneously. Lab School's parents began to perceive the complexity of learning; all aspects of the child's body are at play at every moment. Growth is revealed as individuals interact with their environment, different for every child, even if they are in the same family. At times during a child's day, one type of development may be of primary significance, as in a playground activity where physical skills of memory and coordination evolve or in a time when a child is exploring in his or her home, at a playground or on the beach. Emotional and social support may be offered to a child seeking new ways to use equipment and toys with supportive language and gestures. Cognitive memories of developing physical skills grow into a foundation for new ways to play on or use different equipment.

Intelligence, for Piaget, is an active process, fueled mainly from within. When parents and caregivers offer appropriate stimulation for their child's stage of development, cognitive skills expand to become aware of even more sensations and more refined learning opportunities. Piaget's ideas have been respected and integrated into educational settings for many generations. Einstein called his friend Piaget's ideas "so simple only a genius could think of it."[20] How children think, rather than facts a child might know, seemed most significant to Piaget. The broad array of choices in each of the Lab School Centers introduced the children and parents to objects for children to explore. The children selected their own materials for play and parents could observe the results of how their child might be thinking.

Matching a parent's expectations and to build upon each behavioral clue their child presented and what the child might be thinking was a goal for Parent Educators as they discussed Piaget's sensorimotor stage of

---

[20] Time. (n.d.). *Child Psychologist Jean Piaget*. Retrieved from https://time.com/archive/6735018/child-psychologist-jean-piaget/

development. Over time, a child's own way of using the toys and equipment during play offers new insight into the child's growing competencies.

As Piaget noted:

"The principal goal of education is to create men who are capable of doing new things, not simply of repeating what other generations have done—men who are creative, inventive and discoverers...to form minds which can be critical, can verify, and not accept everything they are offered...pupils who are active, who learn early to find out by themselves, partly by their own spontaneous activity and partly through materials we set up for them; who learn early to tell what is verifiable and what is simply the first idea to come to them."[21]

How Barbara Young's Developmental Task Inventory (DTI) reflects and complements Piaget's Stages of Development.

With the creation of the Developmental Task Inventory, Barbara Young added descriptions of tasks or physiological processes that reflect Piaget's stages of sensory/motor and cognitive behaviors. She included Coordination, Emotional Development, Socialization, both Visual and Auditory Perception and Memory, Receiving and Expressing Language, and the Thinking categories, which are all factors that support the cognitive realm.

The children did not pass or fail the items observed. These skills were recorded in three levels, "beginning, sometimes, and always," to note the sequence of a child's skills. A sample checklist was posted for all to see. A 3-5-year-old child's individual checklist with teacher and parent educator comments was discussed during parent conferences. The items on the DTI suggested specific new experiences most useful for any child's overall development.

Being quiet and sitting still was **not** a Lab School goal! Communication and language among both adults and children enabled the children to manage their behavior in all aspects of their development, physically, emotionally, socially, and cognitively. Parents developed observation skills and learned and discussed with

---

[21] Piaget J. (1953). The Origins of Intelligence in Children. New York, NY: W. W. Norton and Company, Inc.

other adults the needs of both adults and children during this first stage of their lives together. Everyone, parents, adults, and children, were learning new skills! The parents' goal to ensure their preschool child was ready for learning to read and to learn math skills in elementary school was best described by focusing on the many foundational and developmental tasks included in the DTI.

Suppose a parent or teacher sought information about a particular skill or level of a child's development. In that case, a teacher might invite their child to go to a special place, perhaps a small table set apart from the centers. Some of the items the teacher used for making evaluations were not used in the centers. An example: one set of shapes included large, medium, and small red circles; one set of large, medium, and small blue triangles; and one set of large, medium, and small green squares. The pieces would be randomly scattered on the table; the teacher would ask the child, "Can you put some of these together, so they belong together?" There were several ways the child could do the task: sort by color, size, or shape. If the child initially sorted by color, the teacher might ask, "Is there another way to put them together?" This cognitive item on the DTI was called "sorts three ways." Typically, children valued this individual time with their teacher!

Contemporary theorist, Dr. Stanley Greenspan's Core Stages of Emotional Thinking and the Development of Cognitive Perceptions

Barbara Young's DTI focused on the physical, emotional, social, and cognitive behaviors that describe development. Stanley Greenspan offers descriptions of more general stages of emotional thinking and how interactions with parents and other children and adults may nurture children's emotional and cognitive behavior. During their interactions with the child, emotional reactions may be influenced directly by the child's physical reactions.

"For example, early in life babies need to learn to relate to other people with warmth and pleasure. Once they can do that, they are able to learn to communicate through body language, facial expressions, and gestures. Then once children can communicate, they are able to learn how to use these ideas to represent their wishes and emotions and to communicate what they want or what they feel. Eventually they learn how to make connections between these ideas and emotions so that they can start developing a more

organized sense of themselves, and so on through the grade-school years. Each stage builds on the previous one. " [22]

The First Five Years: Milestones [23]

Self-regulation: be calm and regulated, control impulses, attentive and focused.

Relationships: relate to parents, peers, group, new adults.

Reality and Fantasy: participate and enjoy make-believe play and appreciate reality.

Communication: use gestures, respond to other's gestures, organize words and ideas to communicate.

While Greenspan's publications were not available during the earliest days of Lab School, a Parent Educator became acquainted with how his ideas enhanced parent understanding and appreciation of the challenges her family experienced every day - particularly during Lab School - and added his publications to the Lab School curriculum. The importance of the opportunities for both self-control and exploration provided by Lab School included many opportunities for children and parents to practice essential skills that are also the foundation for the bond and cognitive development of parent and child and their family.

[22] Greenspan, Stanley, M.D., <u>Playground Politics</u>, Addison-Wesley, Reading, Mass. 1993, p. 2
[23] Greenspan, Stanley, M.D., <u>Playground Politics</u>, Addison-Wesley, Reading, Mass. 1993, p. 302-3

Nurturing Bonding and Self-Regulation through Feeding
How Feeding Behaviors and Cognitive Awareness of Safety Strengthen Connections

The cognitive awareness of both parent and child in the bonding and self-regulation process may be influenced by how smoothly the infant feeding process proceeds. Sensory aspects of some of the difficulties in feeding a child may be a digestive, a bodily issue, or a sucking, external, chewing, or swallowing issue. Parents may become frustrated with feeding issues during infancy and with older children. Parents question their own behaviors as well as how they think about their connection with their child; why does what seems to satisfy the child at one feeding but not at another? Parents of infants who experienced difficulties in feeding their child gained support and empathy from other mothers in the infant group. New ideas about feeding rituals and patterns from the other mothers who had overcome some feeding difficulties were heard and valued.

Difficult feeding behaviors in infants may begin with an infant's cry that seems inconsolable; some call it colic. It may be triggered by any sensory process, smell, taste, texture, or sucking and digestive processes, or perhaps an allergy. Sorting out the potential causes of a baby's cry became a problem for the infant's parents to understand. Some new parents' first response was to interpret a baby's cry as hunger or digestive distress. If the baby does not calm with the offer of food, the mother may lose confidence in her idea of what her baby needs. At the same time, the baby's immature sensory processing may cause the baby to become overloaded with unmet needs or unknown factors, including allergies. A new mother's dwindling confidence in her nurturing abilities along with her awareness of her child's pain and difficult sensory experiences, may become caught in a web of self- blame. The child's body may be producing unseen or unknown factors like allergy or digestive issues that produce pain related to specific foods.

The new opportunity for discussions among the parents offered support to those parents caught in challenges with feeding their child, especially as parents of slightly older babies described how time, patience, and maturation often are the only way a feeding issue may be resolved. Parents' support for one another within their infant class lowered stress levels of all.

With a new awareness of allergies in current times, parents can find medical help that was less available during the early years of Lab School. The morning and evening Lab School classes provided a safe place for parents to explore their doubts about their nurturing powers as well as celebrating even simple successes.

Infant class mothers often sought information from each other about issues related to feeding their new baby. A mother in one class shared a way she and her husband created a routine that seemed to satisfy all in the family to feel successful in feeding their baby. She called their routine the "five o'clock bottle." She was breast-feeding their baby, but she suggested her husband give the baby a bottle of formula or breast milk when he came home from work every day, quite predictably around five o'clock. He agreed and both father and child began to experience a new sense of their bond similar to what she experienced as she breast-fed their baby.

He found the time he spent with their son was a way to put work issues aside and enjoy nurturing their child, creating their bond. She also gained some moments for herself, knowing her baby was with his father, both getting their needs met. The baby had the opportunity to experience his bond with his father in a new and predictable way. Everyone celebrated their family bonds, both emotional and cognitive.

Infant massage training also became part of the infant class, giving parents and children a new way to bond with each other over simple physical contact.

An Infant massage practitioner taught nurse and parent educators along with parents in the morning Lab School Infant Classes the use of various oils, how to position the child and a variety of hand movements, as well as conversation during massage, how to interpret a child's responses, a sequence of body parts to follow, choosing appropriate time for a massage. Many parents found joy for themselves through the eye contact and tactile sensations created with their child, and an awareness of how to note subtle changes in movements when the child expressed comfort or distress, or even anticipation of the mother's movements. This tactile sensory experience was also recommended to parents of older children. The calm that often accompanies massage soothes a child and parent in many ways. They become accustomed to both the physical and emotional benefits.

A child's food refusal may test the child's relationships within the family and with other adults. As the child's cognitive development grows from Piaget's sensorimotor stage into the Pre-operational Stage, likes and dislikes become more verbal refusals rather than the cries and withdrawal reactions of the earlier stages. Relationships can grow or suffer when a child refuses offerings that present a dilemma for parents. Greenspan describes this behavior as "testing," or an effort at self-regulation. Those who become picky eaters, or who won't eat anything "juicy with chunks" or of a particular color, smell, or texture present a dilemma for parents: did a child seem picky about choices of food based on some sensory awareness or is some other developmental issue at play? Is the refusal based on social awareness of the power of choice?

Parents wonder will the child ever begin to accept only what is available? Even adults have strong thoughts and opinions about what they are willing to eat. Refusals to eat what is offered may have many side issues related to the child's development. Parents found resources in other parents as they shared their own eating/feeding issues. Contemporary knowledge related to food allergies, especially peanut allergy, was not available in the early days of Lab School. Some allergies are now quickly identified with available treatment that provides relief for the child and parents.

Snack time in the 3–5-year-old Lab School classes provided a glimpse of how sensory and cognitive issues may accompany a child's early feeding experiences. As a child's memory and cognition develop, snack foods provided information and discussion about the taste, colors, shapes, textures, amounts, and numbers of food choices. With parents providing snacks, the choices were different almost every day. Conversations at the snack table broadened the children's awareness of ideas like same, and different, shapes, textures, and amounts. Children also learned how to pour from a pitcher and to set the table with cups and napkins. Conversations at the snack table went beyond the food to include where they had played that day along with ideas developing during snack time for play in the interest areas.

Some food refusals may have arisen from what seem to be both a cognitive and a sensory issue.

At snack time, Ricky loudly complained, "I don't like this snack!!! An adult said, "I'm glad you know what you like and what you don't like. Nobody has to eat a snack they don't like." Ricky asked, "What can I have?" "We only have apple slices and juice today." "Well, I don't like that either." "Okay, you don't have to eat that either." "Okay, you don't have to eat apple slices either. Would you like water?" "I don't like apple slices because they are mushy and look brown." The mother added. "Charles is putting peanut butter on his apple slices. It looks brown, too." "Hmmm...can I try that?" Charles passed the peanut butter to Ricky, who spread it on an apple slice. Ricky said, "I like this. It's good." When he knew the brown stuff was peanut butter, it was ok! Perhaps his acquaintance with peanut butter was only between slices of bread, where he did not see it! Ricky's reaction to simply refusing the offer of food changed with cognitive information: he did not have to eat what he did not like, nor drink what he did not want; he could try peanut butter on apple slices, and the name of the brown stuff was peanut butter.

Accepting refusals like Ricky's "I don't like that!" gave Ricky a new sense of power when Lab School's educators and parents took a moment to explore the child's many senses: visual, auditory/hearing, tactile, coordination, and motor skills, all the physical and emotional/social and development processes needed to embrace the social and cognitive learning offered at school.

However, our first messages describing the play-based environment of the school did not stress academic learning; self-awareness and sensory issues are a foundation for cognitive processes. Any moment that engaged a child might nurture sensory factors inviting self-control, competence and confidence, the social and emotional growth that were primary cognitive goals for children of all ages. Cognition arises as a child's maturing sensory and physical systems learn about and adapt to the sensory offerings of the environment.

Understanding Sensory Responses in Children
How Parents Recognize the Role of Tactile, Auditory, and Visual Cues in Shaping Reactions to Stimuli as Depicted in the Developmental Task Inventory.

Cognitive milestones may be observed and nurtured with variations in how a child uses a toy or equipment and how the adults communicate with the child. The range of equipment and activities available during Lab School mornings enabled each child to use the equipment in whatever way the child's skills, interests, and abilities were developing; toddlers and five-year-olds used the block area in significantly different ways, from simple stacks of 2 or 3 blocks to elaborate castles with moats. Some puzzles were available for older infants, but others proved difficult even for parents who sometimes called on children who loved puzzles for help! Nurturing adults offered reliable help for whatever level of the child's physical, emotional, social, and cognitive development they might manage. Joint problem solving occurred as adults and children communicated to reach solutions. All cognitive development!

Cognitive development through conversations and language stimulation occurred everywhere, among the children and between children and adults, about whatever play activities and development were in progress. Children were observed during all classes as they interacted with the environment and other children. Their parents were developing observation skills and discussed whatever the children might be experiencing with other parents, sharing new awareness of development as it happened.

The invitation for cognitive growth was intrinsic in the toys and equipment provided by the Lab School. Parents became acquainted with the many behaviors noted on the DTI and learned to read a description of children's behaviors from the lower lines of the DTI that led to the "thinking" or cognitive behaviors in the to the top line. Specific activities might be created to observe each child's growth in physical, social, visual and auditory competencies that provide the foundation for thinking and cognitive behaviors.

With the awareness of the foundations for cognitive development provided by the Developmental Task Inventory, a parent described taking her toddler to a golf course for the child to practice walking independently. After the course was closed for the day, the child was able to experience the sensory differences that lead to being able to balance when walking in sand and grass, on both flat and rolling grassy terrains, with descriptive words for each change of surface, each physical challenge. Without holding the parent's hand, falling and getting himself up independently provided experience in adjusting to changes in visual and tactile senses and created a sense of independence and competence for future sensory exploration challenges. Important cognitive skills arise from "baby steps!" along with the words, tones, gestures, postures, and facial expressions communicated between parent and child to further enrich the family bond.

Greenspan suggests that communication between parents and children is an important early stage for developing relationships that a child experiences. The Lab School adults observed and talked with the children during play with toys or activities that stimulate specific physical, social/emotional, cognitive, and language responses suggested by the child's development. The parents were learning the behaviors typical of the sensory-motor and pre-operational stages, as described by Piaget and the DTI. Adults invited new sensory and motor experiences to offer their children through information from guest educators as well as other parents, particularly in the toddler and 3-5 age groups.

Daily Lab School routines offered many opportunities to master sorting, fine motor, visual and auditory experiences. For instance, the" Matching Shapes" skill could be noticed as adults and children replaced blocks on the shelves, set the table for a pretend meal, or did a puzzle. They eagerly shared the challenges and successes in each other's children's cognitive growth, encouraging one another. Competence and confidence were goals for both children and parents!

Parents also began to recognize the knowledge they gained about how communication with a child might be more effective when the adult's eye contact was at the child's level, as Greenspan described in his "Floor Time" video. Children were able to think more clearly, and parents were more aware of their children's emotional aspects.

These ideas often showed up in daily Lab School experiences. Understanding child development theories helps parents see challenging behaviors as part of healthy growth. When parents recognize a child's refusal as complex, they can offer new choices and self-management opportunities. Daily choices at school supported children's physical, emotional, language, and cognitive growth. Varied, repeated activities met sensory needs and encouraged learning, while new relationships and play options spurred further development.

Teaching the Meaning of the Word Safe to Children
How Parents Communicate and Foster Understanding of This Crucial Emotional and Cognitive Concept

Physical and emotional safety were two ideas that staff and parents sought to introduce to their children. Adults were all responsible for ensuring the children's safety and teaching them to manage their behavior and the meaning of the word "safe." Personal safety is critical for both physical and emotional survival. Parent classes were an essential part of creating an environment for safety during the school day and for building confidence in parents as caregivers for each other's children.

New ideas about safety happened every school day. The three Lab School rules reflected a broad view of the concept of choice with clear expectations that children are capable of beginning to learn and to distinguish between safe and unsafe choices. Adult supervision readily at hand gave the children words and a concrete awareness of the meaning of the words "safe" and "choice", lifetime skills.

> *"That is not a choice; throwing blocks can hurt someone! Blocks are for building!"*

> *"What a good choice! I'm glad you asked me to tie your shoe, so you don't trip on the shoelace, fall down, and hurt yourself."*

Physical safety, an idea for both children and parents to remember, was fundamental in the creation of a safe environment. Emotions of fear were recognized and protected while encouraging new cognitive development to help children recognize both safe and unsafe behaviors. Physical safety was a priority for adults to both monitor and define related to different situations. The playgrounds at the different schools were quite different, posing different safety concerns. Some were fenced. Those that were not carefully stationed parents to keep children from wandering away from the safety of the group. Creative thinking on the part of parents expanded safe options available to the children. Sometimes the playground equipment became an elaborate obstacle course with specific directions for how to use each piece of equipment. Parents planned work sessions for themselves to fix fences, locks, playground equipment. The churches valued the parents' contributions.

Emotional safety, along with problem-solving, acceptance of language for all feelings, and strategies for managing one's own feelings were ongoing practices. Evening parent classes provided opportunities for parents to explore their emotions around both the children's and their own adult behaviors. They posed questions about interactions and emotions they had observed. A parent's anger over a child hurting another was accepted by other parents and children. Fears about physical challenges were approached as the parents and children gained an awareness of small steps to reach a goal safely. Sadness over any loss was comforted and validated. Joy was celebrated and recognized as new obstacles were overcome. Simple words like "mad, sad, and glad" attached to infant sounds and babbling, built new memories related to emotions that contribute to a child's knowledge.

Simple memories precede knowledge and intelligence. As a child's growing needs and abilities are evident, it is seldom a change in just physical, emotional/social, or cognitive information and skills. Knowledge happens at all ages, all levels of development; Lab School's parents learned new concepts about accepting children's fears as well as introducing new behaviors to ensure safety that may be within the child's capabilities. Safety is a concept, an idea critical to survival and learning.

 Some cognitive activities might begin during infancy and seem to synchronize position in space and language. Activities were enhanced by supportive adult contact and later with language that added verbal cues about bodily movement. Infant class activities included moments described by the early months in Greenspan's as Stage Three: Developing intentional communication (3-10 months). Singing and rhythmic activities added whole group activities to the new experiences of each parent and infant. Every parent seemed to know traditional songs like "Here We Go Round the Mulberry Bush." Pop Goes the Weasel," "London Bridge Is Falling Down." One parent had learned this song was popularized during the Great Plague and wondered if we really wanted to be singing it. Another opportunity to discuss both individual and societal values.

Another example of intentional communication associated with the physical, tactile, vestibular, proprioception, and auditory stimulation and processing occurred with motions in the activity "Up, Down, All Around..." described as parents moved the infant's body parts to match the words about positions like "Up, down, all around, out, in, and tickle your chin." The song that challenged parents more than three- and four-year-olds, "Johnny works with one hammer..." required independent movements of both adults and children that were sometimes more difficult for the parents than the older children!

Evidence of Stanley Greenspan's Stage 4: Emergence of an organized sense of self (9-18 months) often began to occur in both infant and toddler classes. The children began independently integrating physical and social development with new choices. Recall the older infant group who explored an unfenced grassy area.

The parents added language, names of the things they found and showed to the children. The parents' curiosity invited the children to seek new things, both same and different, to see and name as one takes a walk, combining cognitive as well as a physical activity. Emotionally separating from their mother in this open space became more evident in some children whose walking skills showed a higher degree of balance and coordination, who wandered further away from others.

Recall the "chase" activity initiated by the toddler-aged children. Their parents valued their child's coordinated running abilities and their joyous shrieks as they ran, all evidence of their maturing bodies integrating with their social, emotional, and cognitive development. Parents were surprised and delighted observers; no adult "taught" the children to create their own chase game. Sometimes a less coordinated child would fall, but typically got up, wanting to continue with the others. This was a game the children could "teach" their parents and siblings, too!

The toddlers were beginning to exhibit an awareness of emotional ideas and communication; they were building upon their movement, verbal and non-verbal language, and awareness that objects exist beyond their actual presence in time and space, the idea of "object permanence." Greenspan describes this process as emotional thinking in a series of stages; Stage 5: Creating Emotional Ideas (3-10 months) and Stage 6: Emotional thinking: the basis for fantasy, reality, and self-esteem (20-48 months). Each stage builds upon and refines later stages. Concepts are frequently built through multisensory processes, cognitive development! Consider this sequence of a child's awareness of separations and object permanence, loss and reunions:

A child can be verbally reassured that parents are away and will come home soon. This idea may be initiated by the game of peek-a-boo, which grows over time into the growth of memory and knowledge. It may begin with an infant reflexively moving its hands to dislodge a scarf or other cloth covering its face. A parent adds language and verbal connection with the word "Boo!" and playfully repeats the whole process; "boo" becomes an early word a toddler might say as the connection, the memory that things disappear but reappear. Hide and go seek might follow with siblings and parents hiding behind a piece of furniture or in another room. Another step in the child's growing awareness that "out of sight does not mean out of mind" happens when a caregiver hears a car noise that means parents may be returning after an absence and asks, "Where's Daddy?" and the child runs to greet the parent, object permanence is beginning to take place. At a later stage of development, the child will be challenged with mathematical theories and symbolic meanings, things not concretely observable but stored in long-term memory, a process that may have begun with a simple game of "peek-a-boo."

The spoken language typically observed around age three, along with a child's fine and gross motor and play skills, gives a context to behaviors parents can observe and begins the parent's understanding of the growth/progress of their child's cognitive development. Parents appreciating that their child is developing typically for their age as the child experiments with their physical skills and reacts with emotions was the first step. Parents also discovered where a particular stimulation might be useful and sought information from each other and from the educators in parent classes. When language is added to actions, more complex thinking is built.

Language links each adult's and each child's sensory awareness to a child's world. Communication and language involve words, tones, feelings, gestures, postures, and facial expressions, visual memories that accompany language. A parent reported a moment when she recognized her child's visual memory was developing.

A two-year-old who remembered seeing his mother put cookies in a high cupboard, pulled a chair over to the cabinet, climbed up, opened the cupboard door, and found he could reach the box of cookies! What parents do is likely to be imitated! Nonverbal communication gives a sobering lesson to parents who want their children to obey limits, rules, and laws, to be kind and loving and to learn new things. Language that matches behavioral expectations is crucial to the understanding of abstract ideas. Control over the cookie jars of life is different at different ages and stages. Putting things out of sight only works for a short time. Memory!

Communicating cognitive concepts derived from new physical skills occurred as the children experienced obstacle courses. Often with a sequence of at least three different gross motor challenges, the obstacle courses were a daily activity option for all ages. The increase in coordination when a child repeats a series of obstacles several times in a row reveals the development of motor planning and motor memory, both aspects of cognitive development! Equipment for the obstacle courses included pieces of carpet, cardboard boxes of many sizes, balance beams, furniture, ladders, etc. A grandparent, learning of the obstacle courses, made a beautiful maple balance beam with two different widths to use as the children's balance matured. The vocabulary parents used might include jumping, hopping, crawling on hands and knees as well as full body down as in the "commando " crawl, balancing, and skipping. A sequence involving the playground equipment might include swings, climbing, balls, crawling into and out of large boxes, crawling through the rungs of a ladder set on its side. A number might be attached to the obstacle, five back and forth swings, travel two rungs on an overhead ladder, jump three times on a small trampoline. Repetition revealed how well the child remembered how to manage the obstacle and how it became easier with each repetition. Parent creativity produced interesting combinations of obstacles!

The obstacles might include jumping, hopping, crawling (on both hands and knees) as well as full body down as in the "commando" crawl, balancing, skipping. A sequence involving the playground equipment might include swings, climbing, balls, crawling into and out of large boxes, crawling through the rugs of a ladder set on its side. A number might be attached to the obstacle (five back and forth swings, travel two rungs on an overhead ladder, jump three times on a small trampoline.) Parent supervision to talk the children through an obstacle was often needed, and sticker "rewards" might be given each time the obstacle course was completed, for repetition often revealed how well the child remembered how to manage the obstacle and how easier it became with each repetition. Parent creativity produced interesting combinations of obstacles!

Words accompanying various movements and positions, (up, down, over, under, both fast and slow, etc.), similar to the massage sessions in the infant classes, were all a part of the communication between parents and children using the obstacle course to expand vocabulary and the sensory knowledge useful in many fine-motor activities. Stickers were sometimes added to name tags for each trip through the obstacle course, providing a counting experience when they reported their morning to their parents at pick-up time. Creative use of the school equipment was not limited to ensuring safety.

The Impact of Cultural Language Differences
How Varied Vocabulary Shapes Understanding and Challenges Perception

A newcomer to school was the source of a whole new set of ideas for the boys about communicating and the meaning of words.

A child and his parents from London, England, moved to our area; the father had a short-term job with a space program contractor. The family found a Lab School near their home. Their four-year-old boy spied the block area and its cars and trucks as his first choice for play. An unplanned teaching/learning moment occurred when several of the other four-year-old boys sought a parent and asked a parent for help! "What is he talking about? He called them a "lorry" when he played with the trucks."

Luckily, that mom knew that "lorry" was the word used for "trucks" in Great Britain. She explained that fact to all the boys, who began to use the words interchangeably as they played together. All the boys learned a new word for the same object. Their play took on a greater sense of fun, using the words truck and lorry interchangeably. Several boys proudly announced their new word to their parents, who came to pick them up after school! International peace prevailed.

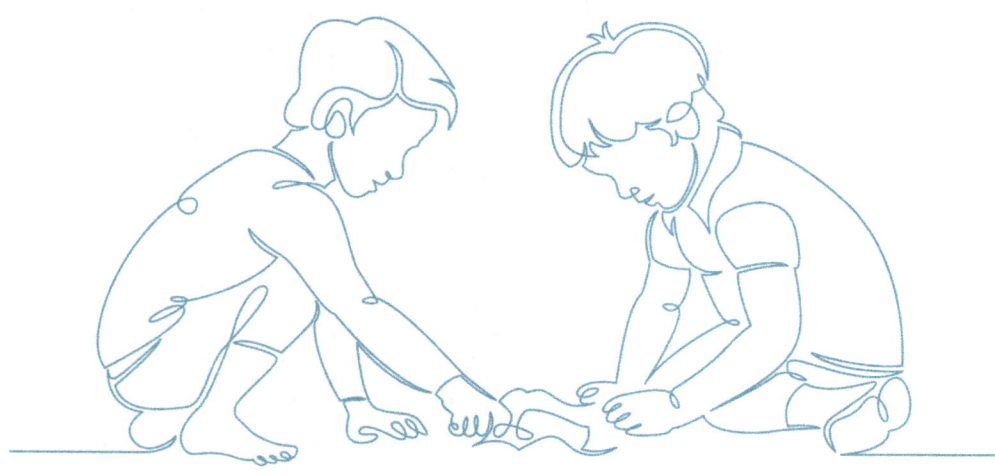

The Power of Non-Verbal Communication
How Thoughts and Ideas Shape Speech and Language Growth in Children

Non-verbal alternatives to spoken language are still valuable before children begin to speak using words to communicate their needs and ideas. Preschool children need time and experiences to help them organize their thinking and to enable them to absorb new information in a group-focused educational setting. One size does not fit all needs.

Cognitive development depends on visual and non-verbal language processing and interpreting an individual's sensory data. Consider the multitude of ways the brain is processing verbal and non-verbal exchanges: sounds, sights, moods, emotions, and physical movement. When parents frequently and meaningfully talk about what is happening in their child's world, they stimulate a child's receptive language. When parents listen to, understand, and respond to an infant's coos and babbles, sounds and movements, they stimulate the child's awareness of language. The parents can observe whether the physical mechanisms of speech and language are intact, functioning in the mouth, neck, chest, and brain. When the parent repeats the child's sounds, especially when they are meaningful to the parent like "mama" or "dada," the infant reveals some knowledge about what it sees and hears, interprets and remembers.

Language and autonomy are intertwined, for only the child can determine when to speak. Consider the power of the moment when Helen Keller first connected the word "water" with the sensation of running water on her hand. Her life story has created new optimism about the potential for those whose physical functioning inhibits the child's communication potential. Non-verbal communication precedes verbal communication in infants; parents often become concerned when a child doesn't speak as much as another child of the same age. Norms for the beginning of specific sounds are usually defined by sounds with a range of ages when the sounds are typically heard from a child.

Infant and toddler classes suggested stimulating the physical structures of the mouth, tongue and breathing, making silly sounds, and adding single words to physical movements. Simply saying, "Up?" rather than "Do you want me to pick you up?" provides a model of simple one-word communication that the very young non-verbal child might begin to say. A child's sense of autonomy builds as both the child's gestures and sounds are understood by a parent.

Another form of communication to use with young children was introduced by a parent who learned sign language when she served as an aide in an elementary school classroom for the deaf. The use of sign language with very young children later became another form of communication to use with young children.

By bringing the ends of the fingers in both hands together means "more" in sign language, and can be useful in communicating, especially with preverbal children. When a child is enjoying a food or an activity and signs "more" you know the child understands the meaning of the word, that he is making a choice. Some parents made up their own signs for use in their own family.

Guest speaker Jane Healy, author of *Your Child's Growing Mind,* spoke to Lab School's parents and the Brevard County community about their important role in their children's language development. She shared:

"Parents are key to developing these sensory opportunities and the language that will communicate both verbally and non-verbally with their child. These early sounds from a child are the beginning of the simple one-word utterances that mark the language of the child's first year of life. When parents experience a child crying and the child responds with its body molding into the comforting arms of the parent, memories, emotional communication, and knowledge are developing. Wordless, tactile, and visual communication become simple and single-word offerings that the baby's auditory senses process and understand, sending information to the memory and intellect that will be defined as the child matures. Any brief exchange, even seconds, may come to be stored into long-term memory. These memories may last a lifetime, ready to be retrieved when useful to the child"[24]

Multi-sensory processing, both auditory and visual, is a vital part of language development. Adults and children communicated most often during Lab School on a one-to-one basis; the Early Childhood Teacher seldom spoke to or directed the whole group. The frequent exchange of ideas shared between adults and children during play was a significant change from what most parents experienced from their own teacher-led school experiences. Preschool children need time and experiences to help them organize their thinking to enable them to absorb new information. When adults frequently communicate to the whole group rather than individual children some children's attention may wander.

---

[24] Brevard Community College, 3.5.1991

Music activities provided a language and auditory experience beyond the conversations during play. A child's xylophone with color coded examples of written music that children used in the Perception center combined visual and auditory skill development. The language of one song was often part of a group music time at the end of the school day. It seemed to find its way into all the 3-5-year-old's Lab School music moments, memorable to both parents and children. Knowledge related to motor coordination, visual, and auditory perceptions were a part of "Johnny Works with One Hammer" sung/chanted by both parents and children as they sat on the floor, feet extended forward. Their fists and heels became the "hammers" to pound the floor rhythmically with the words of the song.

Johnny works with one hammer, one hammer, one hammer, Johnny works with one hammer, then he works with two...

Johnny works with two hammers, two hammers, two hammers, Johnny works with two hammers, then he works with three (use the foot's heel as the third "hammer")

Johnny works with three hammers, three hammers, three hammers, Johnny works with three hammers, then he works with four....

Johnny works with four hammers, four hammers, four hammers. Johnny works with four hammers, then we all go home!

By the time two hands and two feet were pounding on the floor, everyone dissolved in laughter about how silly we all felt and looked. The children were more adept at the motions than the adults for whom the movements were a greater challenge! Four-year-old children gained new awareness of the number four! Physical, emotional, social, and cognitive all at play, an amusing way for parents and children to laugh together.

Empowering Cognitive Growth in Children
The Language Parents Use to Foster Self-Awareness and Cognitive Development

The power of language builds thinking and self-esteem, a means for understanding and controlling one's life. The language parents were encouraged to use, as they recognized the children's efforts in any play activity, sought to describe and define the child's play rather than value it as "good work" or "nice job." Cognitive ideas associated with their play became the language patterns parents learned to use:

- Ask questions a child can easily answer.
- Catch yourself! Don't do anything <u>for</u> a child that the child can do <u>independently</u>!
- When offering choices:
  - *Offer choices that can safely be met.*
  - *"Do you want to choose something to do, or would you like to sit here and watch or rest?" A discussion might occur if a child wants to be alone or rest: "How long do you need to rest? Where would you like to lie down or sit? Let me know when you want to make another choice."*
  - *"Which one first, the big book or the little one?"*
- Language in the Perception area:
  - *"Do you want to do the puzzle all by yourself or would you like someone else to do it with you?"*
- Language at snack time:
  - *"Would you like one cracker or two? A square cracker or a round one?"*
  - *"Do you want juice or water to drink?"*
- Language in the art area:
  - *"You used six markers in your picture, red, yellow, blue, brown, black, and green!" pointing at each color.*
  - *"You made the crayon go here and here and there up and down and across." tracing the movement of the crayon over the paper.*
  - *"What happens when you paint with both blue and yellow? What changes?*

- Language in the block area:
  - *"How many; what is bigger, smaller, same?"*
  - *"That block tower is very tall. What might happen if you put one more block on top?"* *"How many have you put in your tower?"*
  - *"Wow, you made those four big blocks balance on a little one!"*
- Language for two children working on a puzzle together:
  - *"I see you are cooperating. Do you know what that big word means?"*
  - *"Who likes to do all the middle pieces? Who likes to do the edges?"*
- Language with a group of children working to put away dishes in the housekeeping/dramatic play area:
  - *"Someone put all the dishes on the shelf in a neat row. Who did that?"*
  - *"Thank you! Now the next person who comes to use them can see them."*
  - *"Where do all the hats and shoes go? You finished clean-up very fast!!"*

The art area included a variety of media that provided different options for vocabulary building, along with sensory experiences. Typically, a child would choose from whatever was on the shelves. Still, the large child-height table was occasionally used for cooking, food preparation, or messy activities that filled the large table. Even putting on the smocks or old T-shirts to protect their clothing provided physical coordination and sensory input.

One of the favorite activities of the Lab School children was finger-painting in the Art Room. Each child sat in a chair at a table with a large piece of finger-paint paper in front of them. The art room parent would ask," Would you like some finger paint? What color, where would you like it?" The child would indicate the placement and ask for the color. "How much paint do you want, one spoonful or two?" The parent would then drop a teaspoon or tablespoon-sized blob of the chosen color in the selected spot. A broad range of different reactions followed: shrieks of delight, squeals of uneasiness, smiles, frowns, curious inspections of a small dab on a finger, and smearing the paint to cover the entire paper.

We learned to consider this from a sensory perspective, the slow-to-warm children typically needed time to feel comfortable with the new sensation, possibly due to their high level of tactile sensitivity. The children who jumped in and applied the paint with abandon were usually the more unpredictable temperaments with a low level of tactile sensitivity and met their tactile receptivity with gusto. Careful observation of a child's behavior informs the observer of important clues to development and reveals the child's understanding of amount and color.

The Role of Verbal Communication in Toilet Training
How Adults' Cognitive Guidance Supports a Child's Developmental Milestone

With many parents available, no specific toileting times were part of the school day. Many of the church's Sunday School rooms had an adjacent bathroom that any child could use independently at any time. Each child had a space or cubby hole to keep a change of clothes or diapers available if needed or if the child was accustomed to wearing them.

The contribution of language to the process of toilet training serves both parent and child well. Parents in the Toddler classes frequently traded information about their successes and challenges. Many skills enable a child to move beyond diapers independently. Berry Brazelton, M.D., suggested multiple guidelines for parents to determine, "When should a child be toilet trained?" Language to name all elements of the process, names for places used for toileting, telling the child what is happening when the child sees the parent using the toilet, a sense of the child's ability to remove and put on clothing are just some of the ideas that describe the many ideas and skills learned in the process.

One mother revealed that her children had never seen her using a toilet, which amazed the other parents in the group! They asked, *"How did you manage that? I never have that kind of privacy!"* When parents recognize the skills (physical, emotional, cognitive, and language) as needing to be well underway, the process can evolve quite naturally. Another mother reported she thought her child had all those skills, but resisted using the bathroom. His curiosity about the new bathroom when the family moved to a new house seemed to make the difference for her child, and he started using it all the time.

Exploring Cognition
The Role of Common Ideas, Abstract Thinking, and Multisensory Processes

Abstract ideas are particularly difficult for very young children. An infant in the preoperational stage grows in awareness of the complex idea that objects exist beyond their actual presence in time and space. A very young child can be reassured that "Mommy or Daddy are away and will come home soon" is an idea that grows over time with a variety of play activities with accompanying language.

Perhaps it is a reflexive movement that prompts the baby's hands to move under a scarf or other cloth covering its face. The caregiver or parent smiles with delight and says "Peek-a-boo" as they see one another, face to face. The game will be repeated at numerous times and places initiated by both parent and child who enjoy the reunification, the memory of their facial expressions. Something similar happens when the child who can crawl or walk and can be engaged to "find Daddy" who is hiding in a different room not far away. He might call his child to add a clue to the game. Again, the excitement of seeing each other as they play hide and seek, taking turns hiding, perhaps involving the simple word. "Boo!" Another step in the child's awareness that "out of sight may not mean out of mind/ memory." At a later stage of development, the child will be challenged with mathematical theories and symbolic meanings, things not concretely observable, stored in long term memory that may have begun with a simple communication game to reinforce memory.

Toddlers independently revealed to their parents how they were integrating physical, cognitive, and social development as their development of their spontaneous chase game captivated the parents. Their children's social connection with the other children, their freedom to make that choice about their play, their parents' view of their child's coordinated running abilities along with their joyous shrieks as they ran—all evidence that their development in physical, social, and emotional development and their memory were becoming coordinated! What delight all around!

The significance of cognitive ideas evident in things the child is experiencing during play, cannot be overestimated. As the infant grows, language enhances its sensory link to the world. The sensory processes accompanying communication and language involve words, tones, feelings, postures, gestures, and facial expressions. If language is heard, made sense of, produced by the physical senses, and processed by the brain, it produces cognitive information, emotions, and complex social interactions. Words supplement a child's sensory ties to its world. If they hear words attached to their experience, they will develop a rich vocabulary.

"Parents are key in developing these sensory opportunities and the language that will communicate both verbally and non-verbally with their child. These early sounds from a child are the beginning of the simple one-word utterances that mark the language of the child's first year of life. When parents experience a child crying and the child responds with its body molding into the comforting arms of the parent, memories, emotional communication, and knowledge are developing. Wordless, tactile, and visual communication become simple and single word offerings that the baby's auditory senses process and understand, sending information into the memory and intellect that will be defined as the child matures. Any brief exchange, even seconds, may come to be stored into long-term memory. These memories may last a lifetime, ready to be retrieved when useful to the child" [25]

A 4-year-old boy working with the teacher revealed a skill beyond the common sorting activity of sorting colors. The children enjoyed these special times with the undivided attention of the Teacher or Parent Educator. His non-verbal skill was accompanied by his ability to describe a difference he noted visually.

The teacher and a four year old boy were sitting side by side at a table with a set of inch cube blocks of several colors, red, blue, green, yellow, and orange. The teacher said, "Find all the blocks that are this color" (holding the orange block, not naming the color.) He chose all the blocks of that color, and she asked the same question as she presented the other colors.

He chose correctly, moving them into a pile. He enjoyed the activity and continued to group the blocks by color but made two different piles of the blue colored blocks. The teacher noted his choices and asked, "Why did you put these together?" He responded by telling and showing her the letter "B" stamped on one side of all the blue blocks in one of his two blue piles. The outline of the letter was not deep or wide and had escaped the teacher's notice in that group of blocks!! His keen visual discrimination of the blocks and his careful handling as he surveyed all sides of all the blue blocks was indeed surprising. Perhaps the inch cube blocks from several sources had been mixed as equipment was shared among the schools.

This discriminating visual skill was first expressed nonverbally and as a surprise to his parents and teachers alike, but his methodical approach to the task was seen in other ways as he played with other

---

[25] Healy. Your Child's Growing Mind or Endangered Minds check in books

materials. His sense of sorting and his concept of the same and different were more complex than the simple concept of sorting by color.

If a parent or teacher sought information about a particular skill or level of a child's development, a teacher might invite their child to go to a "special place," perhaps a small table set apart from the centers. Some of the items the teacher used for making evaluations were not used in the centers. An example: one set of shapes included large, medium, and small red circles; one set of large, medium, and small blue triangles; and one set of large, medium, and small green squares. The pieces would be randomly scattered on the table; the Teacher would ask the child: "Can you put some of these together, so they belong together?" There were several ways the child could do the task, sort by color, size, or shape. This cognitive item on the DTI was called "sorts three ways." Typically, the children valued their individual time with the Teacher!

A child's choices can be a significant resource for assessing a child's development. If a child avoided play in an interest area, the teacher or parent educator might make observations for specific items on the inventory that prompted that child's choice. The spoken language typically observed in children by age three, along with a child's motor and play skills, also helped parents understand the progress of a child's development, to appreciate their child was developing typically for their age. Parents and teachers often discovered areas where a particular sort of stimulation might be useful.

By communicating with words that describe facts and details in the child's environment, parents build a store of receptive language in their child, valuable information for a child's developing cognitive powers. Early words spoken by infants are often associated with physical characteristics and/or actions or names of people and objects, such as calling for "mama" or "dada", asking for "up, down, in, out," giving names of objects, actions, and people, other one-word utterances meaningful in the child's environment like the words and motions "pat, pat" to replace hair pulling or hitting. The Lab School morning included learning and remembering names of other children, adults, and toys and, through the repetition of songs and games with rhythmic qualities like "Row, Row, Row Your Boat," "Up, Down All Around," "All Around the Mulberry Bush," "London Bridge."

Toddlers might begin to express two words and combinations, say "mine" and pretend by making animal sounds, car and truck noises, express physical needs for types of food or activity and words and sounds describing pain. A child between two and three years old hears words that are particularly important to describe the process of toilet training, a skill that combines physical, emotional, social, and cognitive awareness that words can describe. Language is a tool for organizing complex tasks. Adult recognition of the need to use simple words and sentences produces more expressive responses from very young children. The quality of the adult-child relationship is an important factor in the production of speech; the more a significant person's words accompany everyday routines in the earliest months, the more the child will vocalize in the second year of its life.

Children in the 3–5-year-old group learned that words are one of the ways they form friendships and new connections with the larger world beyond their home. Language was a social tool as children made friends and emotional connections! They learned names; to simplify adult names, we used just first names, sometimes with an honorific. In the eyes of the child, there were adults and children at school. Adults provided safety and assistance to the children during play. They heard words to describe what they could choose to do and what their limits were in a new environment. Language was a tool for creating safety.

It is interesting to contemplate the nature of the relationships between children and adults in Lab School. While the children's safety was a primary responsibility of all adults during the school day, children also had permission to learn new skills, ideas, and words from many caring adults was an ongoing process.

The acquisition of language empowers children to be able to speak for themselves and for others to understand what they know or need or want. Problem solving relies on language for the needs of all who are experiencing conflicts; only safety emergencies require action before words, typically removing a child from a difficult situation or environment! A child running near where children are swinging, who doesn't realize the threat of another child on a swing, might need to be picked up and moved by a nearby adult!

Unlocking the Power of Language through Books
How Reading Opportunities Broadened Children's Understanding and Appreciation of Language at Lab School

Lab School valued the child's auditory, social, emotional, and cognitive experience with books. We read in small groups of three or four children who had each chosen a book or two from the school library. Books were available at any time in the morning as well as in small groups, often at the end of the day. A volunteer "Library Parent" in each 3-5-year-old group supplied books from the public library that were available to the children at any time during the morning. If you visited the school during reading time at

the end of the day when parents were arriving to pick up their child, you would see small groups who might be listening to one another discussing what the book was about, what they heard and saw. Parents learned not only the joy of the information in the books but the value of promoting reading and conversation during the relaxed moments at the end of the day. Everyone could see the book without straining to watch the book and the person reading.

Labels and names provided another opportunity to give meaning to the printed word. Nametags were essential at the beginning of the year when everyone needed to learn each other's names. They were also used to teach concepts and create small groups by using a particular color or shape for a group. Toy shelves might be labeled to promote organization of the materials.

One Lab School borrowed a method called "Plan-Do-Review" from the High Scope Preschool in Ypsilanti, Michigan, a program noted for its long-term success in preventing dropouts and other social problems in the teen years. The Lab School designated one parent who would be assigned several children and asked them at the beginning of the day what areas of play they planned to use that day. The parent would observe where the child spent time at play, and ask each child at the end of the day what he or she had done during their time at school, showing the child what she had written as their plan earlier that morning. There was no requirement that the child should follow his or her original plan. The simple activity of the child seeing their words written as they planned and remembered their school day demonstrated another message about the power of words.

Four and five-year-old children often begin to recognize some words and names, but Lab School emphasized reading as a normal activity during play rather than a separate skill to be taught. Lab School sought to create a solid foundation for each child to manage their needs and behavior in a group setting and as they physically grow and communicate with others beyond their family. Although a few Lab School children had discovered how to read, a focus on reading would come later. Emphasizing verbal communication between children and adults is particularly important to the basic and simple challenges of living in our complex world and as a means to evaluate the cognitive development of the child.

Empowering Children to Navigate Challenges
How Lab School Adults Supported Kids in Managing Behaviors and Building Stronger Communication with Peers and Adults

A Lab school parent struggling to understand why her child seemed more difficult than others found a book called *The Difficult Child* by Stanley Turecki. She asked her parent educator what she thought of his ideas. The result: Dr. Turecki was invited to speak to Lab School's parents! He suggested that some behaviors made children seem more difficult than others. Some children's parents identified "difficult" characteristics in their own child; some even recognized their own "difficult" moments. His ideas provided a tool for parents to understand and help a child whose responses indicated his sensory system was having difficulty adapting to new information.

Those simple three rules the parents learned in their first night meeting produced questions about what to do when children do not obey the rules. One strategy was to define the sensory processes during difficult behaviors. Taking time and addressing the moment through verbal problem-solving was the answer. There are moments with a child when the parent needed to physically remove the child from an unsafe place or moment, such as when a child might run in the area where children were using the swings, but most of the time, a conversation defining the needs of both the individual and group became a problem-solving time. One child usually ran instead of walking when inside.

> **A major function of the brain is learning.**
>
> 1. **Sensory integration**
>   - Taking information through the senses (sight, hearing, touch, taste, smell, and balance)
>   - Organizing and interpreting the information accurately and efficiently
>
> 2. **Remembering**
>
> 3. **Motor planning**
>   - Controlling the body efficiently so as to complete a desired motor act

One child, Joey, regularly arrived at school with his activity level at full speed. He ran through the rooms with little regard for the activities the other children were busy with; he seemed not to notice objects, people or changes. He often called them to join him. Rarely did they even look up, occasionally, one would call back, "No, not now." Upon closer observation, he actually seemed unable to slow himself down, focus on his surroundings, or relate to others, and even looked a bit lonely.

The Teacher stopped in front of him, said in a neutral, emotional, but firm tone, with direct eye contact, and one hand on each shoulder, making physical contact with the child. "Joey, I want to talk to you." Loudly, he replied, "I don't want to talk to you!" "You don't have to talk to me. You can decide that. What are the three rules to remember when you come to school?" He responded, "Don't hurt others, stay where there is an adult, don't call names." "That's right. Good for you. Are you hurting others?" "No." "Are you calling names?" "No." "Are you staying where there is an adult?" Pause...The teacher remained in physical contact with her hands on his shoulders as they talked. "What are you doing?" "Running" "You are right again! Running inside is not safe. You may run into someone. Someone may step in your path. Someone may get hurt. Take my hand, let's look around, and you pick an activity. If you feel you need to run, we will find a mom who will take you to the playground where running is safe."

He chose an art activity of cutting paper into small pieces. The Teacher told the children at the Art Table, "Joey is choosing to cut paper. Thanks for making room for him." Cutting paper proved to be a physical outlet he enjoyed playfully.

With support and time, Joey learned to focus and choose. With practice, he was able to slow himself down, focus, and think more clearly. Difficult temperaments need support as the body adjusts and adapts. Learning to be aware and make choices is an important first step. His high activity level, distractibility, intensity, irregularity, negative persistence, and low sensory threshold were all at play.

We were modeling a technique valuable for a lifetime. Another factor might be found in a child's sensory responses that produce "difficult" behaviors; those behaviors might be desensitized, redirected positively for the child, cognitively understood, and discussed. Some children might seem more difficult for some parents, resulting in a new self-awareness in a parent. Which party was difficult? Or were both?

Turecki suggested that "in a general way, any child may be assessed in each area as follows:[26]

TEMPERAMENT TRAIT	EASY	DIFFICULT
ACTIVITY LEVEL	LOW	HIGH
DISTRACTIBILITY	LOW	HIGH
INTENSITY	LOW	HIGH
REGULARITY	REGULAR	IRREGULAR
NEGATIVE PERSISTENCE	LOW	HIGH
SENSORY THRESHOLD	HIGH	LOW
APPROACH/WITHDRAWAL	APPROACH	WITHDRAW
ADAPTABILITY	GOOD	POOR
MOOD	POSITIVE	NEGATIVE

Language for feelings, words that describe the child's emotions during difficult moments as a child displays difficult behaviors, is a positive alternative or fertile ground for building a child's verbal competencies and vocabulary. Children and adults need simple words in difficult moments to define emotions like "angry or mad, sad, and afraid or scared". Central to the exchanges between adults and children during Lab School problem-solving moments were the simple words that began the child's awareness of the complicated sensory signals that may be a part of the problem or situation the child was experiencing. "Safe" and "hurt" are other abstract ideas accompanying emotional discussions. Using words rather than actions, finding new words to use for feelings can help expand and solve discussions about problems.

Some difficult situations may seem minor to adults but not to children or might not be related to all the characteristics defined as difficult.

---

[26] Tonner, L., & Turecki, S. (1989). *The Difficult Child* (p. 15). New York: Bantam Books.

A parent arrived late to pick up her child, Helen, the only child left with the teacher. Helen looks anxious and sad. "Where is my mom?" The teacher responds, "I don't know. She will probably be here soon." Helen asks, "Why isn't she here now?" "She can tell us why when she gets here." "Why is she late?" "I don't know. Let's give her a little more time. Has she ever not picked you up?" "No, but I don't like her to be late." "Do you feel all alone?" "No, you are here." "Yes, I am, and I will stay with you until your mom comes. Do you want to sit here and wait or help me finish cleaning up?" "I would rather help you."

Mom arrived a few minutes later. "Sorry I'm late! The child responded, "I didn't like it when you were late, but I helped Miss Linda and it was fun."

"Difficult" may stem from what seem to be simple cognitive, vocabulary, and/or sensory issues, as we saw in the vignette of Ricky, who complained the snacks available had difficulties beyond the juice and the apple slice, a combination of all three cognitive issues. He revised his thoughts, spread peanut butter on his apple slices, and experimented with different flavors and textures. Informed choices promote cognition!

Parents need to navigate differences between their own tendencies and learned expectations, and recognize the needs of their different human, immature children. It is a slow, steady slog with no shortcuts. But as parents learned, they adjusted their behaviors, language, emotional responses, and perceptions.

Understanding temperament was especially important to enable adults to modify their own behaviors. The more successful parents develop what Thomas and Chess call the goodness of fit. It is not "giving in" to a child to make such modifications.

An adult was reading a book to several children. Each child selected a book to be read to the group. One child started to fidget and distract the child next to him.

"Vincent, are you getting tired of listening to this story?" Vincent, "Yes, I don't want to hear anymore." "Would you rather work on a puzzle?" "No, I want to go outside." "There is no one on the playground right now. You may quietly work a puzzle or pick another book to look at while we finish this story. You may not distract the others from listening."

Vincent got up, picked out another book and sat down nearby to look at his book, while the group finished listening to the adult who was reading to them.

Even parents described their own difficulty around some Lab School activities. Some of the parents were afraid to supervise the making of play dough until they saw it was something the children could safely manage with simple language related to the steps of the activity. Their fears were accepted and other parents, who felt they could manage the activity so that no children would be hurt, traded workday assignments when cooking playdough was the activity planned for a parent's assignment in the art area.

The children and an adult measured the ingredients (flour, salt, cooking oil, water) into an electric fry pan. The adult explained that after the ingredients were stirred, the pan would get hot and burn them if they touched it. It was important to fear the hot temperature, but that was also when they could control their body. They could keep themselves safe! Stirring the ingredients while the dough was cooking could be done, one person at a time, using a spoon or spatula with a long handle so their hand would be far from the hot surface. Some children were eager to stir, some only wanted to watch. They would take turns doing the stirring. When the mixture stiffened into the play dough, it was turned out of the pan onto the table's surface. As the dough cooled, the children experienced the change in temperature from hot to warm to cool. Colors with food coloring of their choice could be added to the dough they kneaded by flattening, collecting into clumps, rolling with their hands, and providing a tactile, visual, and cognitive experience of changes.

The small group of 3 or 4 children could safely experience making something they liked to use in play. The words for emotions, in this instance, scary, afraid, and fear, associated with the heat of the electric skillet, can be associated with any new experience that a child can learn to manage successfully. The parents who did not like to oversee making play-dough had an opportunity for them to explore their fears so they might better help their child learn new ways of managing their feelings as new skills were developing.

Some parents of the older children had developed cooking activities at home. Consider the fine motor skills developed as one learns to crack an egg, pour liquid from a pitcher or watering can, spread peanut butter for a sandwich, or butter bread to make a grilled cheese sandwich. Parents sometimes provided snacks at school with children actively involved in the preparation, especially when only the older children attended. One mother found some small plastic pitchers so every child could pour juice. It was a bit messy initially, but children learned quickly to pour efficiently.

Understanding and Addressing Difficult Moments
Early Childhood Knowledge Guides Parents in Problem-Solving and Cognitive Growth

While information about a child's history, emotional, and social development could be important in the problem-solving process, cognitive development was also significant.

Jane, an adopted child:

The temperament trait of a relatively easy child related to "approach/withdrawal" was brought to the parent educator by the child's mother:

Jane and her adoptive parents had first met when she was almost one year old. She was born in a foreign country. Her physical development had progressed along the typical sequence during the years after adoption and before she came to the 3–5-year-old Lab School class. She readily adapted to the other children and their parents and the school routine and verbalized her needs. After several months in school, her mother asked the parent educator about Jane's willingness to approach other adults and give them hugs, including those she had never seen before in public places like the shopping mall. "Is that normal?" her mother wondered. The parent educator reviewed with her the sequence of early attachment, bonding, and awareness of strangers that often or typically happens during the infant's first year. The mother knew Jane had been in nine foster placements prior to being adopted and she realized that Jane needed to learn what a stranger might be. The mother was afraid that Jane might have long term challenges if she did not experience and learn the difference between family and strangers.

Because Jane's cognitive development had progressed along typical stages, several options were discussed that might address the issue. The parents might use the words "stranger" and "family" to define different relationships in everyday experiences. She might begin by asking Jane for hugs at specific times when the family was together, such as when anyone was arriving or leaving from home. When the mother brought up the challenge In parent class, other families were willing to share their experiences during the time their children were displaying stranger awareness and/or anxiety. Protecting Jane from dangerous situations related to strangers began with strengthening her attachment to her parents.

Chaos!!! Identical twins from two different families in one Lab School class.

One Lab School group met a very difficult challenge when two families with identical twin girls joined a 3-5 year old group. Imagine two sets of identical twins in a group of sixteen other preschoolers! The overwhelmed parents of each family with twins needed, sought, and found support from the whole group of parents, whose empathy and challenging experience during their initial contact with the twin girls motivated their willingness to help. They were overwhelmed by the twins, too! Everyone found them to be difficult! Everyone wanted help!

The parents of the twins discovered their two families experienced their children's first years in remarkably similar ways. No one could tell the siblings apart! Stanley Turecki's definition of "temperamentally difficult" describes these four girls.

After many questions and much discussion in a parent night meeting, the whole group became involved in planning how to deal with the twins as individuals.

According to both sets of parents, none of the four children slept for more than one hour at a time and awakened with loud, inconsolable protests. They resisted the comfort offered them. Parents were stunned by the difficulty in managing these difficult temperamental live wires. The twins appeared to overstimulate each other, and the households were plunged into extraordinary noise and chaos due to temperament, high activity level, high distractibility, high intensity, irregularity, high negative persistence, low sensory threshold, withdrawal, poor adaptability, negative mood. "Double trouble!" not "double fun" as the old Double mint gum jingle put it. After the parent meeting, all the parents became involved in using the following strategies were that were implemented in the school day:

1. Each twin selected a different outfit to wear to school.   No more identical dresses or outfits. Even the girl's own parents needed help in identifying each girl.

2. Upon arriving at school, each twin (and all the   other children as well) would go to a parent who was writing names on name tags and watch as the parent spelled out the child's name as she slowly printed it on a name tag for each child to wear.

3. Accompanied by an adult, each twin then selected a play area to start her school day. The other children chose their activity independently as they had been doing all along.

4. The parent in the area chosen by each or the four girl twins would make eye contact, lower their tone of voice, gesture toward possible choice of activities, name and describe the activity. For example, "We are doing finger painting today: What color do you want to use? Or would you like markers and paper or Playdoh?"

Providing a structure for all parents to use was a start. The outcome was a source of relief and encouragement for the twins and their parents, as well as the other Lab School parents. After several weeks at school following this routine, the four girl's behavior gradually calmed; the other children continued to follow the routine they were used to, all still choosing activities they wanted to explore. All four twins became able to and interested in making choices. They also spent more time involved in focused activities and play.

At home, their parents reported a calmer, less stressful household gradually evolved over several months. The twins' parents began to feel more successful at managing their Herculean task! It didn't happen overnight, but all the parents were relieved. The difference between managing and their own behavior with the twin's. By focusing on verbal communication about the choices each girl was making, the twins' individuality was reinforced. Each twin had time to process the new experience and feel comfortable with the opportunity. The other children continued to follow their more independent choices.

Changes in the twins' school environment provided the support needed by their sensory systems to begin to reach a degree of calm that they were missing. Their parents had been unable to adapt to the high levels of stimulation generated by each girl's interactions with her twin. When that level was lowered, each system, family and school, was able to respond more efficiently. The reduced input allowed time for a response and feedback for the next step. Each child began to experience her individuality. The adults in the children's lives, both at home and at school, gained a consistency that built the children's sense of self that very gradually became a sense of self-control.

Jeff: a family mourning his mother's death.

Another family came to Lab School on the recommendation of a family already enrolled. The fathers knew each other from work. Tragically, the child's mother had died from an incurable condition during his infancy. Jeff was almost 4 years old. Extended family members had cared for Jeff during his mother's illness and when his father was at work. His father had married again, and Jeff's stepmother recognized that Jeff had missed some early development stages. He had very limited play skills, was not toilet trained, and ate only a few kinds of food. He was not disruptive but did not readily join activities, choosing to play by himself, frequently lying on the floor with objects he could spin or move with his hands. His temperament traits related to sensory threshold, approach/withdrawal, adaptability, and mood all seemed at play.

Jeff was watching the other children on the playground when the parent educator kneeled to gain eye contact with him and asked, "Do you see those boys on the swings? Would you like to swing sometime?" When one of the boys left his swing, she asked, "You could sit on my lap like you have done when we read a book, and we could swing together." She offered a hand, which he accepted, and they walked to the swing. She sat on the swing and lifted him onto her lap. "Put your hands here (showing her own hands on the swing's chains) and hold on like I am doing." She put her hands over his but moved them away as he held onto the chain, then moved the swing very slowly, making the swing go back and forth. His body began to relax. "Tell me when you want to get down, and I'll help you. We can let go of the chain and get off the swing." After a short time, he said, "Down." Each day, they repeated these steps when he accepted an invitation to swing, noting that adult prompting was unnecessary as he gained comfort with the motion and slowly initiated the process himself.

The parent educator had gradually moved how she sat on the swing so that Jeff was sitting directly on the swing seat, not on her lap. "I think you are ready to swing all by yourself, Jeff," the parent educator said several days later. He nodded in agreement and gradually mastered independently getting on and off the swing and enjoying the motion.

Lab School adults gently encouraged Jeff to try new activities in different sensory environments, gradually expanding his choices. When faced with something new, Jeff learned to ask for help, which staff and parents supported. His slow-to-warm temperament and visual processing shaped his willingness to explore. Parents adapted by offering gentle, varied sensory input and celebrating his progress. He gained protection, permission, and growing confidence. Occupational therapy was recommended as he moved into elementary school. Though his family moved away, Jeff remained a bit slow-to-warm but was now more communicative and optimistic. When parents understand and support their child's unique needs, guiding behavior and communication becomes easier, helping the child's brain grow and adapt.

Embracing Creativity in Lab School
How Unique Behaviors and Expressions Were Supported and Encouraged

Jessica: a knowledgeable clown-to-be.

Four-year-old Jessica and her mother arrived at school and were greeted by their Parent Educator. Jessica looked at the Parent Educator and excitedly exclaimed, "OOH, you look like a clown!" The Parent Educator responded, "I feel like a clown! My new curly hairstyle is very different and I'm just getting used to it." Jessica's mother had a distressed look on her face as Jessica moved into the school to choose an activity. "I am so embarrassed!" her mother said. "No need to be embarrassed! I'm amazed she noticed!" replied the Parent Educator. Her mom added, "You need to know Jessica has been very curious about clowns lately and thinks she wants to be a clown for Halloween. She couldn't have given you a more heartfelt compliment." The Parent Educator responded with information about how young children are often afraid of clowns as well as the Easter Bunny and Santa Claus because they move like humans but look so very different, and often do not speak. Her mother explained that her father had asked a co-worker who was a member of a clown club if she would allow Jessica to observe her as she put on her clown costume and makeup. Jessica was quite impressed by the process she witnessed.

The parent and Parent Educator shared the whole story with the parents who were working at school that day, delighting in Jessica's observation and insight. This transformation vividly demonstrated her new cognitive ability to "hold previous concepts" in her thinking, an important skill when reading and math will be offered in elementary school.

The Parent Educator couldn't have created a better example of this thinking skill. The mother could save a discussion about whether someone might have considered "you look like a clown" in an uncomplimentary way for another time. The two adults laughed over the whole conversation; the Parent Educator complimented her mother for hearing Jessica's ideas and helping her understand the nature of clowns. Jessica had not expressed fears about clowns, a common reaction in young children. Her visual perceptions and memory reflected her growing cognitive development. Her comment also provided a glimpse of social awareness and a good chuckle for her mother and the parent educator as they shared the story with the other moms present that day. Pretend play expands a child's cognition in many ways: ideas, identities, concepts, language, recognition of differences between reality and fantasy.

Older boys pretending to be *Power Rangers*.

One group of older four-year-olds provided challenges to their teacher, particularly related to safety. At times they would physically act out with each other the movements like the strong and powerful characters they saw on *Power Rangers*, a popular television show at that time that involved lots of physical kicking and punching. She took them aside one day and told them she wanted to have a meeting and talk about "POWER." They loved the idea. Cognitive idea!

> She said, "I can tell you all really like power. Let's talk about what powerful things you can do as four-year-old boys." They replied, "I can run fast!" "I can climb up and jump down!" She replied, "Yeah, that's great. How about with your mind, your brain? You can think, and when you know things, you can be very powerful in making choices and decisions. Let's think about the choices you have here at school." They replied, "I can decide what to do in the Block area, and what I want my art project to look like, and who I want to play with." She said, "Yes," adding, "When we follow those ideas and rules, you have a lot of power because you are using your mind to make choices, right? What happens when you make a choice not to follow the rules?" They replied, "Usually the adults or someone tells us to stop." She added, "So we know that when you use your mind and follow the rules and are in charge of your body, you keep your power, but if you don't follow the rules and play in an unsafe way, you can lose your power and the adult has to be in charge of you. So how are you going to keep your power?" They replied, "Follow the rules!!"

The older boys in most 3–5-year-old classes seemed to delight in their physicality, much to the concern of parents of younger children. The boys were typically drawn to active play that the group sometimes organized, but they did not avoid other areas or centers for play. Their parents came to appreciate that their physical coordination found an outlet during the school morning while they were also developing social skills and self-awareness. They often enjoyed cooking activities, which developed planning, communication among adults and children, sorting, and fine motor challenges in measuring ingredients. And eating the results! More power!!

Patrick: a creative thinker during pretend play!

Patrick presented complex skills, creativity, and cognitive abilities beyond most of the children in his Lab School.

A Parent Educator noticed a 3 1/2-year-old boy standing at an easel, painting while looking out a window at a typical flat Florida landscape of one-story houses with dark roofs. He was wearing a red dress that he had chosen from the dress-up clothes rack. While painting, he kept looking out the window as though he were painting what he saw. The adult said, "This is such an interesting picture. What are those?" pointing to large triangular shaped objects in the back of the picture, the roofs of the houses. In a high falsetto voice, he said, "Those are mountains." She asked, "Mountains?" "Yes, that is the way they look from here. This is the house where Little Red Riding Hood's grandmother lives," pointing to the middle of the picture. "I am Little Red Riding Hood today." He continued until his painting was finished then moved on to another activity.

All morning he continued to use his Little Red Riding Hood voice and pretended to be that well-known character. At the snack table, another child asked, "Why are you talking like that?" He answered matter-of-factly, "I am Little Red Riding Hood today." Snack time continued without further comment from his friends. Pretending is a common preschooler's creative outlet! When snack time was over, he moved to go out to the playground, still in the long red evening dress. A parent stopped him at the door and reminded him that dress-up clothes stayed inside. "But I want to wear it the rest of the day." "You can do that," she told him. "Just remember that the dress-ups stay inside." "Okay," he acknowledged. He did and chose to play with blocks, another favorite activity, continuing to wear the red dress.

When his mother came to pick him up at the end of the school day, he was still in the red dress, speaking in his Little Red Riding Hood voice. "Wait a minute until I put this up," he said to her as he rehung the red dress. He told his mom, "I was Little Red Riding Hood today." "That sounds like fun," she replied. " I wonder who you will be tomorrow?" "I don't know. I'll think about it."

He chose an idea, perhaps from hearing a story, developed many aspects of the idea, and wove them into role-play and pretending during his whole morning at school. He never once forgot to use the special Little Red Riding Hood high-pitched voice. Organized thinking, pretend play, memory of a story, social confidence, choice, sense of time, awareness of limits, time to expand his creative mind with support for his thinking, his ability to express himself in words and actions! Competent and creative, not difficult in any way!

Elizabeth: an organized and assertive authority on drinking fountains.

An older four-year-old, Elizabeth, was thirsty. She climbed the step stool to reach the water fountain, pushed the button for water to come out and loudly announced, "Will somebody please come help me push this button. It doesn't work right!" Indeed, it required a strong push to bring forth the stream of water; the children had seen and talked with the custodian for the church who had worked to fix it numerous times. Assertive Elizabeth knew adults were within the sound of her voice and she was impatient and thirsty! She was accustomed to asking for and receiving help when needed; she was quite self-sufficient in all areas of development. Her mother heard her and remarked, smiling, "Isn't that just like Elizabeth?" Indeed, the button was often difficult to engage; Elizabeth knew how to solve this problem and many others as well!. She thanked the adult who came to help and took off for the playground through the door next to the drinking fountain.

Remember Robbie, the young three-year-old who was too short to reach the water and sought to "bend" the water to get a drink. When Robbie announced he was "bending water," his thinking process included how the water moved out of the hole when he pressed the lever. He also knew he couldn't reach it with his mouth to get a drink. He had reached the top of the steps used to climb up to reach the water. He knew the word "bending." While his idea to get the water to "bend" seems amusing today, perhaps his vocabulary and thinking were missing other words and thoughts about how he might reach the flowing water with his mouth. His freedom to choose his activities was in full force, and he knew he needed to climb to reach the water and turn it on. His initiative and self-control were in play, even as a young three-year-old. When children have the cognitive power to choose their activities, they reveal development in an individual way that gives the adults in their life a sense of other things, including how the water moved out of the hole when he pressed the lever. He also knew he couldn't reach it with his mouth. He was becoming a problem solver!

A different problem with a drinking fountain, a different level of development, in a place where children learned to and believed they could solve problems, with adults for help and guidance when needed.

"It can very well be that a method or an approach which works with one child will have no effect upon another, if the method is not geared to the personality needs of the second child..."

Selma Fraiberg

Afterword

The Lab School experience has left a lasting impression on generations of families, fostering a deep sense of connection and growth that endures long after childhood.

What a wonderful variety of children and their families were part of the Lab Schools! When we meet many years later, it seems that nothing has changed in the parents' sense of their Lab School experience, even though their children are now independent adults. The Lab School bond is intact. These parents hope creative thinkers will continue to find new ways to meet young children's and their families' needs.

May this Lab School story inspire new ideas for early childhood education, designed to meet our children's and their world's needs. Educators and the community may find ways to create classroom cultures where children explore, make choices, solve problems, and learn to appreciate others. Adults may realize that traditional classroom cultures may not offer these opportunities, while parents can see how childhood play fosters healthy family development.

Lab School modeled physical, emotional, and social development and supported children's growing abilities to make choices about play, solve problems, develop skills, and respect others. Parent education provided opportunities to practice supporting and nurturing their children during preschool. As a Dad offered in a night meeting for parents, 'we are in this program for our children, to offer them an enriched opportunity to learn. They do become more competent and confident, but we parents benefit most - we become more competent and confident.'

May all adults, parents, extended family members, elementary and secondary school educators, and employers of parents with young children recognize how children's play, when nurtured by adults who recognize that making choices and managing their behavior during play is a valuable and significant resource for a lifetime of learning. The Lab School culture provided these foundations for treating many learning challenges that may prevent children from fully realizing their potential.

Barbara Young retired in 1985 and moved with John back to Seattle. Their children are now spread across the country. For Barbara's eightieth birthday, family and friends gathered at her daughter's home, enjoying music and lively political discussions around a fire-pit. Each person voiced their candidate choice, met by cheers and groans. Smiling at the spirited crowd, Barbara remarked, "A noisy bunch, aren't they?"—a reflection of her appreciation for individuality and the impact she had on us all.

Acknowledgements

Our worlds have been surrounded by people who loved, supported, and believed in us - our families, husbands, children, friends, professors, and mentors - even though one was challenging, one quiet and thoughtful. Every child needs such a support system - those who love, laugh, cry, and hold limits firm while enjoying each other and their many differences.

Most recently, we thank Mariane Brillante, Susan Riebsame, and Claire Peffer, former Lab School personnel who read and remembered their experiences; many thanks to Jane Young Arthur, Joy Patterson, and Theresa Morgan. Most importantly, we thank all the Lab School families who provided these memories.

About the Authors

Suzanne Geier, Ed.D., LMFT

Geier earned a BA from Duke University with a major in psychology and a minor in philosophy, an MS from Florida Technological University (now the University of Central Florida) in psychology, and an Ed. D. from Nova University in educational administration. She was Barbara Young's second Lab School teacher, became a parent educator, and was the program's director when she retired. She spent her professional life working with children and families.

She and her husband, Bill, an electrical engineer in the space program's early days, lived on the Indian River in Rockledge with their two children. Now retired, she enjoys cooking, the outdoors, engaging with others, and community involvement.

Wendy Potter, MA, LMHC

Potter earned a BA in English from the University of Michigan and taught English in high school until her first child was born. She and her husband, Bill, moved to Brevard County, where Bill, a new attorney, decided to establish a practice. Following the recommendation of a friend, they enrolled in the Lab School program.

While in Lab School, Wendy earned an MA in Guidance and Counseling through Stetson University. As Lab School reflected what she was learning in the Stetson program, the Potters continued Lab School with all three children. Wendy became a Parent Educator for all four age groups: Younger Infants, Older Infants, Toddlers, and Three to Five Year Olds.

The close-knit Potter family now has three children and three grandchildren. Their experience within their own family and contact all these years later with former Lab School parents affirms the effect of Lab School on their children's adult lives, a generational effect.

Wendy and Bill now split their time between Montana and Florida, where they enjoy changes in terrain and temperature. In retirement, Wendy, who has a 'green thumb', digs being a Master Gardener.

Appendix

List of Guest Speakers

Burton White, Ph.D.
The First Three Years of Life, Prentice Hall, Paramus NJ, 1975
Encouraged parents to appreciate their roles as the first and most important teachers in their child's life.

Jane Holmes, PhD.
Developmental Neuropyschological Assessment, Dyslexia: a Neurolinguistic Study of of Traumatic and Developmental Disorders of Reading,1973.
A research psychologist shared her knowledge regarding brain and neurological development of the fetus.

John Dusay, MD.
Egograms (Transactional Analysis) Bantam Books, 1960
A psychiatrist discussed transactional analysis and his pictorial representations of ego states.

Jane Healey, Ph.D.
Endangered Minds, Simon & Schuster, 1991
An educator and author, spoke to the enormous influence of parents on the lives of their young children with appreciation for the language they use.

Stanley Turecki, M.D.
The Difficult Child, 1985
A psychiatrist helped parents understand their child's behavior as a function of temperament and develop more effective strategies.

Taibi Kahler, Ph.D.
Process Communication, Transactional Analysis Revisited, Human Development Publications, Little Rock, Ark, 1978
A psychologist explained how interactions between parents and between parent and child reflected different needs and perceptions.

Lucy Miller, Ph.D, OTR
Miller Assessment for Preschoolers, 1983. American Journal of Occupational Therapy, May 1983
Spoke to Parent Educators and Teachers about using her Miller Assessment for Preschoolers as an easy tool for assessing preschoolers' overall functioning. Brevard County School System was invited to send personnel.

Bibliography

Ainsworth, M. (1979). Infant-mother attachment. American Psychologist, 34, 932-937.

Ayres, A. J. (1976). Sensory integration and the child. Western Psychological Services.

Babcock, R. N. D. E., & Keepers, P. D. T. D. (1976). Raising kids OK: Transactional analysis in human growth and development. Grove Press.

Bowlby, J. (1958). The nature of the child's tie to his mother. E. H. Baker & Co.

Bowlby, J. (1968-1972). Attachment. Basic Books/Tavistock Institute of Human Relations.

Brazelton, T. B. (1984). To listen to a child: Understanding the normal problems of growing up. Da Capo Press.

Briggs, D. C. (1975). Your child's self-esteem: The key to life. Paperback.

Cannon, W. B. (1915). Bodily changes in pain, hunger, fear, and rage: An account of recent researches into the function of emotional excitement. Appleton-Century-Crofts.

Dusay, J. (1960). Egograms (Transactional Analysis). Bantam Books.

Dusay, J. M. (1980). Egograms: How I see you and you see me. Bantam.

Elkind, D. (2015). Giants in the nursery: A biographical history of developmentally appropriate practice. Redleaf Press.

Erikson, E. H. (1950). Childhood and society. W. W. Norton & Co.

Erikson, E. H. (1982). The life cycle completed. W. W. Norton & Company.

Fraiberg, S. H. (1959). The magic years. Scribner.

Frohm, E. (1956). The art of loving. Continuum International Publishing Group.

Galinsky, E. (1987). The six stages of parenthood. Addison-Wesley.

Gesell, A., & Ilg, F. L. (1949). Child development: An introduction to the study of human growth. Harper.

Greenspan, S., & Greenspan, N. T. (1985). First feelings. Viking Adult.

Groder, M. (1977). Asklepieion: An integration of psychotherapies. In Transactional analysis after Eric Berne: Teachings and practices of three TA schools. Harper and Row.

Hanley, J. R., Hastie, K., & Kay, J. (1992). Developmental surface dyslexia and dysgraphia: An orthographic processing impairment. The Quarterly Journal of Experimental Psychology Section A. https://doi.org/10.1080/02724989243000046

Healy, J. M. (1990). Endangered minds: Why our children don't think. Simon & Schuster.

Healy, J. M. (1999). Endangered minds. Simon & Schuster.

Holmes, J. (1973). Developmental neuropsychological assessment: Dyslexia—A neurolinguistic study of traumatic and developmental disorders of reading. University of Edinburgh.

Ilg, F., & Ames, L. B. (1966). Child behavior. Perennial Library, Harper and Row.

Ilg, F. L., Ames, L. B., & Baker, S. M. (1992). Child behavior: The classic child care manual from the Gesell Institute of Human Development (Revised edition). MorrowPb.

James, M., & Jongeward, D. (1972). Born to win: Transactional analysis with Gestalt experiments. Da Capo Press.

Kahler, T. (1978). Transactional analysis revisited. Human Development Publications.

Maslow, A. (1943). A theory of human motivation. Psychological Review, 50, 370-396.

Maslow, A. (1954). Motivation and personality. Harper & Row.

Miller, L. (1983). Miller's assessment of preschoolers. American Journal of Occupational Therapy.

Papalia, D. E. (1979). A child's world: Infancy through adolescence (2nd edition). McGraw-Hill.

Papalia, D., & Olds, S. W. (1972). A child's world. McGraw-Hill.

Papert, S. (n.d.). [Profile of Jean Piaget]. Retrieved from http://www.time.com/time/time100/scientist/profile/piaget.html

Perry Preschool Study. (n.d.). HighScope Educational Research.

Piaget, J. (1952). The origins of intelligence in children (M. Cook, Trans.). International Universities Press.

Piaget, J. (1954). The construction of reality in the child (M. Cook, Trans.). Basic Books.

Restak, R. (1990). The mind. Simon & Schuster.

Restak, R. (1991). The brain has a mind of its own. Harmony Books.

Restak, R. (2003). The new brain. Rodale.

Rogers, C. (1961). On becoming a person. Harper Inc.

Rowan, J. (2016, March 2). Perspectiva.

Santrock, J. W. (1983). Life span development. W. C. Brown.

Smart, M. S., & Smart, R. C. (1970). Children's development and relationships. The Macmillan Co.

Smart, M. S., & Smart, R. C. (1972). Children. MacMillan and Co.

Thomas, A., & Chess, S. (1977). Temperament and development. Brunner/Mazel.

Thomas, A., & Chess, S. (1987). Know your child. Basic Books.

Thomas, A., Chess, S., & Birch, H. (1970). The origin of personality. Scientific American, 233, 102-109.

Turecki, S. (1985). The difficult child. Bantam Books.

White, B. (1975a). The first three years. Prentice-Hall.

White, B. (1975b). The first three years of life. Prentice-Hall.

Winnicott, D. W. (1992). Babies and their mothers. Hachette Books.

Winnicott, D. W. (1994). Babies and their mothers. Hachette Books.

Young, B. (n.d.). [Personal communication].

Developmental Task Inventory

DEVELOPMENTAL TASK INVENTORY [Part One]						LEVEL I	
THINKING						Sorts One Way	Uses One-to-One Correspondence
EXPRESSING LANGUAGE			States Physical Needs	Asks Questions		Counts to Ten	Gives Opposites
RECEIVING LANGUAGE			Recognizes Day & Night	Understands Simple Commands		Understands Position	Recognizes Color
AUDITORY MEMORY			Performs Commands 2	Repeats Words		Repeats Simple Sentences	Performs Commands 3
AUDITORY DISCRIMINATION			Hearing Screening Results	Responds to Sound		Discriminates Between Common Sounds	Identifies Common Sounds
VISUAL MEMORY			Recalls Animal Pictures	Patterns Pegboard Beads		Names Object from Memory	Recalls & Replaces Objects
VISUAL PERCEPTION		Matches Color Object	Matches Form Objects	Matches Pictures		Matches Size Object	Matches Size & Form
EYE-HAND COORDINATION	Follow Target w/Eyes	Strings Bead	Copies a Circle	Buttons & Fingerpaints		Cuts with Scissors	Copies a Cross
SOCIALIZATION	Relates to Family	Indicates Wants [Not Cry]	Toliets Self	Washes and Dries Hands	Dress Self	Separates from Mother	Relates to Teacher
EMOTIONAL DEVELOPMENT	Withdraws at Strangers	Withdraws at Frustration	Cries at Frustration	Combats Frustration	Displays Emotions	Expresses Emotion Physically	Verbalizes Emotion
COORDINATION	Creeps	Walks	Runs	Jumps	Climbs	Hops	Balances on One Foot

NAME _____ DATE _____

BIRTHDATE _____ LAB SCHOOL _____

PARENT EDUCATOR _____

TEACHER _____

ALWAYS

SOMETIMES (BEGINNING)

NEVER

NOT ATTEMPTED

DEVELOPMENTAL TASK INVENTORY [Part Two]	LEVEL II		LEVEL III			LEVEL IV			
THINKING	Orders Sticks by Length	Order Heaviness Sequence	Order Size Sequence	Holds Previous Concept	Compares Size and Number	Sorts Two Ways	Recognizes Difference	Orders Numbers	Sorts Three Ways
EXPRESSING LANGUAGE	Names Animals	Comprehends Remote Events	Defines Words	Describes Common Objects	Builds Sentences				
RECEIVING LANGUAGE	Understands Function	Knows Body Parts	Relates Words to Picture	Comprehends Directional Command	Recognizes Tense				
AUDITORY MEMORY	Repeats 7-8 word Sentence	Repeats Clapping Sequence	Repeats 4 Numbers	Recalls Story Facts	Repeats Numbers				
AUDITORY DISCRIMINATION	Locates Source of Sound	Hearing Differences Between Words	Matches Rhyming Sound	Matches Beginning Sounds	Matches Ending Sounds				
VISUAL MEMORY	Recalls Color Sequence	Reproduces Design from Memory	Recalls Picture Sequence	Recalls Part Design	Recalls Word Forms				
VISUAL PERCEPTION	Matches Direction of Design	Matches Numbers	Matches Letters	Isolates Visual Images	Visual Perception				
EYE-HAND COORDINATION	Copies a Square	Copies a Triangle	Copies Symbols	Copies Divided Rectangle	Copies a Diamond				
SOCIALIZATION	Relates to Parent	Relates to Group	Takes Turns	Plays with Group	Relates to Stranger				
EMOTIONAL DEVELOPMENT	Sucks Thumb Masterbates	Feelings of Shame	Feelings of Pity	Feelings of Self-Esteem	Sense of Humor				
COORDINATION	Catches & Bounces	Skips	Balances on Walking Beam	Jumps Rope Assisted	Jumps Rope Alone				

Brevard Community College

LAB SCHOOL GUIDEBOOK FOR PARENTS

A PLACE TO GROW

LAB SCHOOL GUIDEBOOK FOR PARENTS

Overview of Program

The Lab School program is for parents from all socioeconomic levels and backgrounds to play, work, and learn together. Through this experience, parents learn to be more competent and confident, and children begin to learn to value themselves and take responsibility for their own behavior. Churches, recognizing an opportunity to strengthen families, have been partners in this process at Brevard Community College. Without their support; BCC could not offer this community service.

lab school is based on the premise that: 1) a parent is the child's most important teacher; ?) the parenting process is learned; 3) the most powerfullearning opportunity is direct involvement that; 4) reinforces existing skills and offers opportunity to develop new strengths; and, 5) that practice is an important aspect of the learning process. Parents in the program are involved, available, and flexible.

This program is for "do-lt-yourselfers", BCC provides the resources and opportunity. What you do with it, depends upon you. You make the decision for yourself and your child.

Each proqram - infant, toddler, preschool - is geared to the developmental needs of the child and the opportunities needed to support growth.

The co-op structure allows for unlimited richness, variablility, and quality. Your program depends upon you as an individual, you as a group. The program is desiqned for parents who are excited about learning, have a willingness to invest themselves, and give themselves permission to take risks and grow. As should be the case, parents benefit more than children.

Appendix/Parent Handbook, continued

. GOALS OF THE PROGRAM

FOR PARENT

1. Will learn about yourself as a person, as a wife or husband and as a parent.

2. Will be able to take an active role in your child's school experience.

3. Will have the benefits of learning with other parents who have children near the same age.

4. Will have an opportunity to consult with trained and qualified persons concerning yourself and your child's development.

FOR THE CHILD

5. To enable each child to become physically healthy, emotionally sound, mentally alert, and socially well adjusted.

6. To help the child mature at her or his *own* pace.

7. To enable the child 10 controlhis or her own body through good coordination and muscular control.

8. To build a positive self-Image in each child.
   a. To see him/herself as a capable learner.
   b. To be responsible for his own acts,

5. To help the child adjust to his or her environment.

6. To help the child develop trust in concerned adults, his laacher, and other children.

OPEN-ENDED ENROLLMENT PERIOD

The Lab School program is "on-going" in that parents may enter the program as meets the needs of the family. The program begins with. BCC's Fall term in late August for parent meetings and the children's program begins the first Wednesday after Labor Day in September. The program closes for the summer on May 31. Call the Division offices, 632-1111, Ext. 3485 to find out if space is available.

GEOGRAPHICAL LOCATIONS

Schoools are located in 8 areas of the county. You are encouraged to participate in the school nearest you. If enrollment is full, you may register in the nearest school with an opening. Discuss any changes with your Parent Educator as changes are disrupting to routines and group cohesiveness.

IDEAL CLASS SIZE

In order to provide a rich learning environment large enough to support program needs and small enough to meet individual needs, the following class sizes are recommended.

Infant groups - 10 families
Toddler groups - 12 families
Preschool groups - 20 families

Note: The term family, here, refers to the child who is participating and the parents. Often, there are single parents, and, often, grandparents support the family by participating. Grandparents, or other care-givers also participate with parents by attending parent-meetings. Discuss this with Parent Educator.

Appendix/Parent Handbook, continued

REGISTRATION
Registration forms may be obtained from the Division office or from the Parent Educator of the class in which you are enrolling. Call 632-1111, Ext. 3485.

As both parents participate in the program, each registers in the program. A completed registration for each parent, with a check for the first and last month's fee is submitted to your Parent Educator.

Give yourself time to look over the form carefully, and fill in all information requested so that your registration can be processed without delay.

BILLING
BCC Accounting Department will bill each family shortly after the 25th of each month. Accuracy of your bill will depend upon accuracy of your participation records.

Check the attendance records posted in each school to see that your participation is acknowledged. If a discrepancy is noted, notify the Parent Educator.

FEES
MONTHLY RATE

Program	Amount
Infants	$5
Toddler - 1 day	$5
2 days	$10
Preschool - 3 days	$15
5 days	$25

Parents each pay a $5 per month registration fee.

WITHDRAWAL
Withdrawal forms may be obtained from the Division office or from the Parent Educator. You will continue to be billed until the Division office receives the withdrawal notice.

PARTICIPATION
The program is designed to focus on the process of parenting through interaction with one child. The experience provides the parent time and opportunity to Qain insight into the unique qualities of that particular child and build a close and effective relationship with a goal to enriching their lives together and separately. A parent whose energies and attention is divided between two siblings simultaneously is unable to respond to the needs of each. Consequently, each program is limited to parents and one child.

Page 4

Parents decide whether this program meets their needs, and in the case of families with more than one preschool aged child, they will decide how best it will do so. The decisions are difficult. Occasionally, parents will decide to participate in two programs with two children and are happy with their decisions. However, double participation requires tremendous energy and commitment. What you learn as a parent generalizes to other children and situations so that most often, parents decide to focus on one child at a time in the program and end up enjoying the process more.

PARTICIPATION REQUIREMENT
Each program is designed to meet the developmental needs of the particular age so that the enrichment and involvement change with the needs of the child.

InfanUParent attend a morning session each week with their child and both parents attend meeting at night once per month.

Toddler/Parent attend a morning session with their child and one or both parents attend meetings twice per month at night.

Preschool/Parent attend a morning session once a week and an evening session three nights per month. Conferences with individual couples are scheduled one night per month on a rotating basis.

Parentswho are unable to attend the meetings of their own groups, extend their knowledge and make up the time by attending another group's meeting.

ATTENDANCE
Regular attendance is expected of all parents. In keeping with college policy, two unexcused absences per term are allowed. Excused absences are illness and out-of-town. Notify Parent Educators of absences. Parents participate in this program by choice and your absence is a cause for concern.

Enthusiasm and commitment is an important part of the Lab Schoo.' spirit. Absences are correlated with a lack of enthusiasm and commitment and negatively influence group process. You are an integral part of the progr~m! With busy schedules, it is important to coordinate your activities so that being involved in parenting is fun and not conflicting.

TEXTBOOKS
Textbooks for each section (Infant, Toddlers, Preschoolers) are ordered through the College Bookstore. Copies are available at all three campuses.

INSURANCE
In agreement with churches allowing us to use their facilities, an insurance policy is purchased through Parents Cooperative Preschools Instructional

Page 5

Appendix/Parent Handbook, continued

(Pcpi) for a nominal fee ($1.25 per family in 1986) to cover accidents while at school. Check with the treasurer of your group if you wish to read the policy.

SCHOLARSHIP FUNDS

For parents who are in financial need, a limited amount of funds are available through the Barbara Young Scholarship Fund which is a part of the BCC Foundation.

Each year, parents in the program participate in a fund raising event to augment the amount of funds.

Should you need help with your tuition, discuss your request with your Parent Educator.

COMMUNITY AWARENESS EVENTS

Several times throughout the year, parents participate in community sponsored events such as fairs and mall displays (i.e., Parenting Fair at Merritt Square Mall, Well Baby Clinic at Holmes Regional, Indian River Festival, Titusville Chamber of Commerce •. etc.).

Interaction with the community promotes awareness of our program, gives the public an opportunity to meet Lab School parents, and provides support for programs that benefit the public.

CLEANUP

Parents are responsible for weekly cleanup and for leaving the facility ready for Sunday. Churches are generous in allowing us the use of a facility in which they have a deep emotional and financial investment. We value this goodwill and leave the premises as requested by the churches. In order to meet this responsibility, close coordination between the Sunday school teachers and BCC church liaison person is essential.

End-of-the-year cleanup will be scheduled. At the end of May equipment will be returned to BCC for storage unless requested otherwise. For example, the Sunday School Teacher may want us to leave the housekeeping equipment or large wooden blocks for use with her class. Also, the rooms used during the year will be repainted as needed in the color approved by the church.

CLEANUP DEPOSIT

A $10 deposit is paid to the group Treasurer at the time of registration and is returned at the year end cleanup. Deposits are forfeited for those not participating in cleanup.

Page 6

SAY "YES" TO LAB SCHOOL!
FAMILY AFFAIR

BCC LAB SCHOOLS

COCOA LAB SCHOOL

COCOA BEACH LAB SCHOOL

INDIAN HARBOUR BEACH LAB SCHOOL

MELBOURNE LAB SCHOOL

MERRITT ISLAND LAB SCHOOL

PALM BAY LAB SCHOOL

ROCKLEDGE LAB SCHOOL

TITUSVILLE LAB SCHOOL

FOR MORE INFORMATION CONTACT:
DR. SUE GEIER • BREVARD COMMUNITY COLLEGE • (305) 632-1111, ext. 4580